Routledge Revivals

Liszt, Wagner and the Princess

Originally published in 1927, this illuminating study concerns three people, about two of whom much has already been written. The third, Princess Carolyne Sayn-Wittgenstein, has attracted less attention, in spite of her having occupied the greater part of Liszt's inner life. The Princess in the large sense was an unmusical woman. It is a question whether her influence over Liszt was of a beneficient nature. She interested herself in Berlioz only for the purpose of checkmating Wagner, whom she hated, and thus set Liszt against Wagner whenever possible. The complex relationships of this inscrutable and not altogether scrupulous trio are here considered for the first time in a way which adds much of value to our estimate of the characters of Wagner and Liszt.

Liszt, Wagner and the Princess

William Wallace

First published in 1927 by Kegan Paul, Trench, Trübner & Co. Ltd

This edition first published in 2024 by Routledge
4 Park Square, Milton Park, Abingdon, Oxon, OX14 4RN

and by Routledge
605 Third Avenue, New York, NY 10158.

Routledge is an imprint of the Taylor & Francis Group, an informa business

© 1927 William Wallace

The right of William Wallace to be identified as the author of this work has been asserted by him in accordance with sections 77 and 78 of the Copyright, Designs and Patents Act 1988.

All rights reserved. No part of this book may be reprinted or reproduced or utilised in any form or by any electronic, mechanical, or other means, now known or hereafter invented, including photocopying and recording, or in any information storage or retrieval system, without permission in writing from the publishers.

ISBN 13: 978-1-032-94209-4 (hbk)
ISBN 13: 978-1-003-56947-3 (ebk)
ISBN 13: 978-1-032-94221-6 (pbk)
Book DOI 10.4324/9781032942094

PLATE I

LISZT

[front.

LISZT, WAGNER, AND THE PRINCESS

BY

WILLIAM WALLACE

Author of *Richard Wagner as He Lived,
The Threshold of Music, The Musical Faculty,
The Conductor and His Forerunners*

WITH FIVE PLATES

LONDON
KEGAN PAUL, TRENCH, TRUBNER & CO. LTD.
J. CURWEN & SONS; LTD.
1927

Made and Printed in Great Britain by
M. F. Robinson & Co. Ltd., at The Library Press, Lowestoft.

CONTENTS

CHAP.		PAGE
	PREFACE	ix
I	1 AMARE ET REDAMARE	1
	2 THE BROAD VIEW	3
II	1 THE WONDER-CHILD	7
	2 THE DÉBUTANT	12
III	ELOPEMENT	18
IV	VAGABOND INDEFATIGABLE	29
V	BÉATRIX—NÉLIDA	44
VI	THE BEETHOVEN MONUMENT	48
VII	ENTER THE PRINCESS	55
VIII	SCHWÄRMEREI	68
IX	WEIMAR DAYS	77
X	VISITS TO WAGNER IN ZURICH	81
XI	WAGNER AGGRIEVED	90
XII	VOX ROMANA	100
XIII	RÖMISCHE BRILLE	109
XIV	ENTER COSIMA	117
XV	LA PRINCESSE CHEZ ELLE	125
XVI	CAUSES INTÉRIEURES—BONDAGE	132
XVII	CAUSES EXTÉRIEURES—RELEASE	147
XVIII	SECRET SERVICE	159
XIX	THE SHRINE	169
XX	THE LAST PILGRIMAGE	179
XXI	FANTASTICS	186
	BIBLIOGRAPHY	189
	INDEX	193

LIST OF ILLUSTRATIONS

PLATE		PAGE
I	LISZT	*Frontispiece*
II	WAGNER IN 1877	82
III	PRINCESS CAROLYNE SAYN-WITTGENSTEIN IN ROME	126
IV	LISZT IN 1886	170
V	PLAY-BILL OF THE HUNDREDTH PERFORMANCE AT BAYREUTH OF *Parsifal*	178

PREFACE

Of recent years there has been a noteworthy effort to get rid of the sloppy sentimentality with which the lives of public men have been deluged. They have not been studied as human beings but as automatons.

The vividness of their work, their enthronement in the mind, have blinded their worshippers to features in character, to idiosyncracies, even to failings. There is no task more disquieting than that of tracing to its source some popular misconception. Ignorance, with its foster-child fanaticism, has thrust aside the cold and impassive analysis of fact, and set up in its place unthinking conclusions based purely upon individual desires and private impressions of what a man must have been to have accomplished what he did.

This frame of mind is the more inveterate the higher the artist stands in his own sphere. However unpalatable truth may be, it nevertheless is truth, and though at times we may not be able to obtain it all, there still remains sufficient to justify an estimate of character.

Preface

The pages that follow concern three people, about two of whom much has been written. The third, Princess Carolyne Sayn-Wittgenstein, has attracted less attention, in spite of her having tenanted if not barricaded the greater part of Liszt's "vie intérieure." The only monograph devoted to her appears to have been Adelheid von Schorn's *Franz Liszt et la Princesse de Sayn-Wittgenstein*, an authorized translation in French from the German. Fraulein von Schorn and her mother had been intimate with the Princess, and had stood by her when Society in Weimar gave her the cold shoulder, but while attempting to be impartial she was more of the Wittgenstein party than of the Liszt party. The tone of the Princess's letter in Chapter XVIII puts beyond doubt her suggestion that Adelheid von Schorn should act as her spy upon Liszt. For, as will appear in the course of this study, there was not always that unanimity between the Princess and the Abbé that has been so readily accepted and believed, or indeed between Wagner and the one or the other. However trustworthy in what it supplies, the preface to this monograph, written by Hughes Imbert, exemplifies very significantly what has been said here in the opening sentences. It is undoubted that in the early years of Liszt's association with the Princess he produced his best work, but he was living in the musical atmosphere that he desired, that stimulated him and fully occupied his mind. But after she went to Rome and laid upon him the burden of answering her interminable inquiries and paying heed to her admonitions, he was out of touch with the world of music that beyond question was his, and was occupying himself with forms of composition, which, profound in their ecclesiastical meaning as they might be to him, were driving him to express himself in an alien and sterile tongue. He was only too conscious of this.

Therefore it is with amazement that we read in M. Imbert's Preface, " La Princesse Wittgenstein fut une femme absolument supérieure : son influence sur des génies tels que Berlioz, Wagner, et Liszt, eut les plus heureux résultats."

It is difficult to see what an utterly unmusical woman had over Liszt in the way of beneficent influence. Over Berlioz it was of a negative kind, and he interested her only for the purpose of checkmating Wagner whom she hated. When she told Berlioz that she would never speak to him again if he did not write his opera, *Les Troyens,* her motive was to encourage the composition of a work which would cast Wagner's into the shade. The Preface quoted was published in 1905, three years after the last volume of La Mara's collection of the Liszt-Wittgenstein correspondence appeared, and therefore within M. Imbert's reach if he had chosen to read between the lines.

It has been thought best, in a general sense, to let each of this strange trio supply the context upon which this book is based. A research of this kind calls for full documentation, and in the short bibliography will be found a few of the works which have proved useful. It is right to mention specially Kapp's invaluable *Life of Liszt*. With its help I have been able to trace events which he has suggested rather than described. In an account of three people who apparently met together in the same room only on the rarest occasions in forty years, it is impossible to adhere to a strict chronological sequence, but dates and references have been given where it has been necessary to show the bearing of one event upon another.

I may perhaps be allowed to intrude at this point with a personal note.

In the course of studying the environment of Liszt and the Princess Carolyne Sayn-Wittgenstein in Rome my interest was quickened by the discovery that as a boy in Rome in the 'Seventies I was actually living under the same roof as she was. A comparison of dates and addresses with those in Liszt's *Letters*, a letter of my own which I still have, and the diary of a near relative kept while I was there, confirm this. This, I believe, will account for my having seen Rome through the " Roman spectacles " [See Chapter XIII] that Liszt saw it.

This brings me to think of all the people that I had

Preface

seen or who had been pointed out to me, from Alexandra, Princess of Wales, with her mother, both unattended, stepping off the pavement to make way for others—from these royal ladies down to Presbyterian ministers and Scottish doctors.

I may have rubbed shoulders with Liszt and the Princess Carolyne in Piale's English Library in the Piazza di Spagna, the leaflet of which is now before me. I was not old enough to have heard of Liszt, but I did know a good deal of the Overture to *Tannhäuser* by heart. I travelled by carriage to Tivoli by the road that Liszt must have covered many a time. I may have lunched in the same room with him in the Locanda della Sibylla, hard by the temple and the waterfall. It and the Fountain of Trevi are mentioned in my old letters. I may have met him in the gardens of the Villa d'Este, probably heeding him no more than I had been heeding the hundreds of his cloth that blackened the streets of the Eternal City. There is a blur here and there, but across these years I can say that I saw Rome as Liszt saw it in the 'Seventies.

We have now to see the three Fantastics in their relationship to one another. The art of Music stands high in the esteem of those who find it most worthy, without regard for the lives of those who conceive it. In this essay we are confronted abruptly with the disconcerting fact that the "poses et mensonges"

—the words applied by Liszt to his ex-mistress, the Countess d'Agoult, the mother of his children, might equally have been applied to the three, to Liszt himself, to Wagner and to the Princess—an inscrutable and not altogether scrupulous trio.

WILLIAM WALLACE.

London, 1927.

LISZT, WAGNER, AND THE PRINCESS

CHAPTER I

I. AMARE ET REDAMARE

IN the friendship between two men there is an interest, an attractiveness begotten of the common spirit of humanity. It is a gift rarely bestowed, rarely exercised. It can never be one-sided. The bearing of another's burden, in honour preferring one another, self-sacrifice, even in the immaterial hindrances of life, most surely go to the welding of the bond. It asks for nothing: nothing expects. It inhabits a mansion of its own erecting, calm and serene. The seeking after personal glory is idle if the glory is not shared by both alike. Loss to the one is a blow to the other: the gain a triumph to each.

Those who pursue friendship in art are nearer the Art of Living than those who pride themselves in their independence, though independence is no poor thing, with a splendour of its own. In quietness and thankfulness there have been occasions when presumings and yieldings have held the scales even. Between man and man, between manliness and manhood, there can be no rift in perfect friendship.

Tradition has handed down the story of great friendships—mythical, authentic, legendary, fictitious. The classical instances have been rendered indestructible by time: less edifying are those of Holy Writ: it is certain that the most perfect have been too sacred to have courted the admiration or curiosity of the world.

Many examples have been held up as worthy of imitation, but of these none is less secure than the friendship between Liszt and Wagner. It was not evenly balanced: strength was not met with strength but with weakness. The brain and hand that took, gave little. The surrender was all on one side. The hallowed name of friendship was desecrated and its serenity darkened. Begun in opportunism it flourished awhile then faded.

In what follows there are still gaps to be closed. These it will be the task of a later generation to fill if ever they can be filled. The purpose here is to examine the attitude of three persons to one another after a study of such documents as are within reach. This is an age of research and these latter years have seen a resolute, an urgent tendency to apply to historic matters the methods with which the man of science pursues his investigations. Just as imagination comes into play in many a biological problem, so too, in an attempt to sound the under currents that determine motives and their accomplishment, imagination tempered with sympathy may discover their abiding purpose.

In the history of music there never was a period more charged with expectancy that that associated with the names of Liszt and Wagner, whether for good or ill time alone will show.

2. THE BROAD VIEW

The aspect of Liszt most fixed in the minds of the past and the present generation is that of a saintly man but for whom we should never have had the miracle of Wagner's music. That miracle sufficiently justified in the opinion of many the claims for his canonization.

In a broad sense the art of music owes to him what Italian art owed to the Medici. There is not a name among musicians, his contemporaries, which at sometime or other was not in his mind, on his lips, or in his heart. With Berlioz and Wagner there is a crowded company of men and women whom he helped, either as composers, in giving their works a hearing and winning over publishers on their behalf, or as performers to whom he gave, or for whom he found, engagements.

But against this splendid company there were others who flattered his complaisance, took advantage of his weakness, of his desire to be on good terms with everybody, and then broke his spirit by their base ingratitude. Foremost had stood Joachim, the opportunist, with Brahms in the background; Schumann sulking and goaded by that gadfly, his wife, though Liszt had discovered the artist in his music long before he had met and had to endure him as a man; Heinrich Heine with his acrid tooth, and—Richard Wagner himself. The dapper Mendelssohn was the jeune premier of the cast.

It was Liszt who provided the money, excepting some negligible subscriptions, for the Beethoven Monument in Bonn. He gave the first performance of *Lohengrin* in spite of inadequate resources; he served Schumann's *Genoveva* on the same plane, giving its first performance which the composer did not choose to attend. For the faith that was in him he encountered a storm by producing for the first time *The Barber of Bagdad*, by Peter Cornelius, a storm directed not against the composer but against himself, and because of that attack he laid down his baton for good as a conductor of opera.

These are instances detached from the records of the Theatre at Weimar while he was conductor-in-chief. In these memorable years he was alert in discovering artists who were not all interpreters.

Chief among them was Berlioz, who again and again was encouraged, beginning with the early days when Liszt transcribed the *Symphonie Fantastique* for piano in order to make it known and accessible. So also was it throughout the career of Berlioz.

At Weimar Liszt's position was difficult. It was a small town, unable to pay large fees to artists, and overshadowed by the superior airs that Leipzig affected. While Weimar held all music for its province, Leipzig was cold and aloof, erecting a standard of art and taste which it declared was not to be impugned. There were two camps. It was perilous to serve Weimar if Leipzig disapproved and closed the doors of its Gewandhaus. War was declared between the Schools in spite of advances held out by Liszt, whose aim was to build the golden bridge in the sacred cause of music. When the gospel of one school is repudiated by that of another, one in the end must prevail. Ultimately there may be room for a gradual and imperceptible coalescence which resolves the two. But at this time differences were acute. How much was due to the personality of the protagonists is not obscure. Take examples— Schumann mentally was heavy and stupid ; Liszt had become too much a man of the world to be driven into argument : besides, there was a vigilant Princess looking on with an eye like a griffin. Joachim was an opportunist, loyal to Liszt when loyalty paid : disloyal when disloyalty paid better. Wagner was parodying in himself the Sermon on the Mount with amendments in his own favour, and Brahms was making etherial flights with wings of homespun.

It was all unspeakably futile, as if theories, opinions and cliques could block the way to the spread of human intelligence.

In the midst stood Liszt, pledged to all that was worthiest, "Zur Hälfte Franziskaner, zur Hälfte Zigeuner," he might say of himself—half monk, half vagrant—in his incessant journeyings over Europe, but that applied more to his earlier life than to what fitly may be called his monumental period, for there was something statuesque, grotesque too—in the second half of his life, which raised him on a pedestal, looking down half-amused, half-sad, upon the human comedy around him. This was the man in his maturity.

CHAPTER II

1. THE WONDER-CHILD

Liszt's disposition for music was shown at an early age and it was bewildering. Fostered and encouraged by his father, himself no narrow-minded amateur, he played in public before he was twelve. He did not find himself stranded at the age of twenty, as so many precocious youths have been. The spark that had been kindling within him was not extinguished, as theirs often was, before they had passed out of their 'teens. His had blazed up into flame, and he was little more than twenty when he had all Europe at his feet. It may be that some rumour of Mozart's career had reached his father's ears, putting him on his guard to play the part that Mozart's father undertook in the case of that prodigy. We may conclude that Adam Liszt did not exploit his son—at any rate, at the outset, for here we have the paradox that the lad seemed unconscious of the power that within him lay, and wished to abandon music and submit himself to the religious life.

Nowadays we should view with no small amount of apprehension this swing of the pendulum, this tendency to go from one extreme to another—from the freedom of the artist's life and thought to self-renunciation and the cloister. Liszt was to have it both ways. There was a moment, imperceptible, but still measurable, when the pendulum hovered between pianist and penitent, virtuoso and voluptuary, and shared its favours impartially. With virtue and strength he was the " virtuoso," hammering the keyboard with the terrible gift that was his, and as he grew older, vain enough to think that he himself was the keyboard upon which womankind strummed *their* " virtuosity."

As a child his first appearance in London was a success. He played at Windsor and was patted on the head by King George IV, who remarked, " I've never heard anything like it in my life." During a second visit to London, from April to June, 1825, at a private concert the flute-player, Alfred Nicholson was about to play a composition of his own, with piano accompaniment, when it was found that the piano was a semitone lower than the tuning of the flute. Some argument passed between Nicholson and Cipriani Potter who was at the piano, and a deadlock seemed unavoidable, when Potter turned to Liszt and asked him if he could transpose from C to C sharp. Liszt, who had already played, at once complied and somewhat improved the piano part.

It was in this year that his one-act Opera, *Don*

Sancho, ou le Château d'Amour, was given at the Paris Opera with orchestration attributed to Paër with whom he was studying composition. Three months after another visit to London, in 1827, Liszt lost his father. By this time, however, he was becoming conscious of contempt for the public, and it was dawning upon him that the platform was not the best field for the cultivation of his artistic sense. Further, his steps were wandering churchwards, and he began to ask himself if the priesthood was not his true vocation. But for the loss of his father this doubt hardly would have arisen, for when the subject had been broached in his father's lifetime he was told to listen to Art and not to the Church. This, and his father's dying words that he feared his son was destined to fall a prey to the entanglements and domination of women, showed how accurately he had forecast the future of the sixteen-year-old lad.

Settled in Paris with his mother, he realized that the scanty savings from his concert-tours would not suffice, and he began to give lessons to aristocratic and wealthy pupils, attracted to him by his reputation as a pianist. To have studied with Liszt in those days had not the import and prestige that it was to gain later. It was nothing short of a twelve hours' day for him, with scanty time to breathe.

Among his pupils was Caroline Saint-Criq, daughter

of the Minister of the Interior. Her invalid mother, when well enough, was present and was gratified to see the dawn of something else than music lessons. Not for the first time was music teacher turned lover. How ever could opera, fiction or drama have fared without the idea? But when the long illness seemed near the end, her mother thought it best to tell her husband, adding that if the pair were in love with one another, she saw no objection to their engagement. The Count merely raised his eyebrows. These things did not happen in the families of Charles the Tenth's Ministers, and the matter was dismissed.

When Liszt arrived for the usual lesson he was told that the Countess had died in the night. Then Caroline entered alone, white as a sheet. They fell into one another's arms, and the lesson continued over a shut piano on poetical and romantic themes, till Liszt was summoned to the Presence. Thanks coldly offered preceded the word of dismissal. Caroline was packed off to a convent according to the mode of the day, there to await preparations for her marriage with Count d'Artigaux. The marriage was an unhappy one. Liszt chanced to meet her again on his way to a concert-tour in the south of France, and for the last time in 1844. In his will of 1860 he remembered her and left her a ring, but she died in 1874, twelve years before his death occurred.

The Wonder-Child

Thus ended Liszt's first and, we may believe, his only real love affair. With other "affairs" in mind it is almost clear that there was something in this on a very different, a loftier plane than those which were to dominate him throughout his life. That he thought of her in his will, thirty-three years later, even under the eye of that other Carolyne, Princess Sayn-Wittgenstein, shows that in the depth of his heart Caroline Saint-Criq held a secret place unprofaned by the all-conquering Aspasias that hammered therein.

In despair Liszt sped to his ghostly counsellor, Abbé Bartin, wounded in his pride, and renewed his supplications to enter into holy orders, but the Abbé, knowing too well his penitent, pointed to music as the better comforter. This panacea, however, did not yield immediate results and for the better part of two years Liszt lay in the toils of some kind of religious melancholy. From this he was roused most effectively by reading his own obituary in *L'Étoile* — an indication of how far he had advanced in his public career. But the necrology did more: it was almost a passport, an introduction not to the Elysian Fields, but to the less visionary and infinitely more mundane Champs Élysées.

2. THE DÉBUTANT

The Paris of the 'Twenties and 'Thirties had not quite the atmosphere into which a youth still in his teens should have been plunged. It was in a grotesque masquerade that Liszt found himself, in which temporary attachments were formed or rent as easily as partners were changed at a ball. Gallantry scarcely veiled, careless, promiscuous, had something of the operatic tenor about it, with storms and protests of love bursting forth into an impassioned flame, to gutter down like a spent candle till a fresh one was lit for the next occasion. The old domino was tossed aside and a glittering foil, as insincerely worn as its predecessor, took the stage till it, too, went. The parade was quite " palais-royal " in its artificiality and ineffectiveness.

If the staircases of many a house in Paris could have spoken, their tale would have been one of effrontery or stealth, with the stair-carpet ostentatious even in its shabbiness, and its invitation, " Essuyez vos pieds, S.V.P." But only to the first floor. Beyond that nothing was of consequence. Then came dark rebellious stairs that creaked even to the light tip-toe beside the heavier tread, betraying by their sound and notifying the tolerant neighbours, *diminuendo*, of another ill-disguised intrigue. A gust of wind and the slamming of a door—then the honest citoyen drowsily turned on his side and fell into a sleep, too deep to notice whether the creaks of the stair were repeated later in a *crescendo* from above.

Doubtless there were instances of conjugal fidelity in the bourgeoisie, but as the painters and musicians, artists and writers, regarded themselves as a class apart and insisted upon the recognition of their claim, they lived above and beyond the moral law as commonly interpreted. Talent and wit might palliate many an irregular and irresponsible union, and even the transfer of affections or a kind of double harness did not always appear to lead to heartbreaks.

Swept into a social set through his gifts, Liszt found himself in a milieu strangely at variance with that cloistered life which not so far back had seemed his true vocation. The abbé that he was to become, some thirty-five or forty years later, was in some respects not unlike the facile and adventurous abbés of the late eighteenth century, whose successors in the nineteenth, but in sadly thinned numbers, strove to uphold the tradition of their caste for gallantry in many a scented boudoir. The powdered wig had fallen and then the head—Louison, with her single tooth aloft, glittering against a leaden sky—then a downward flash. But that was ancient history, a couple of decades before Liszt, on the twenty-second of October, 1811, saw the light. Memories had become dulled.

In the first chapter it was suggested that Liszt had earned grace in the eye of the public under some secular rite of canonization, and we have been informed on good authority that not a few saints had their legends of mis-spent youth, wild lives and death-bed repentances. In these cases there always was work for the Devil's Advocate. Liszt's record, even for the latter part of his days, was no legend, for there was many a hysterical woman who flung herself across his path.

He was now to be so closely associated with France, with French thought and language, that French became almost his mother-tongue and supplanted his native Hungarian. We are not told, however, what language he employed in conversation with his mother, the daughter of a dealer in hardware at Krems, a small place on the Danube above Vienna. German he was to pick up later, and he was aware of his defects when in writing to Uhlig in his fortieth year he spoke of his effort to patch up more or less skilfully his very halting German.

He now found himself developing ideas somewhat at variance with the sacerdotal mood through which he had just passed. Much sought after as a pianist, and coming in contact with the most brilliant, and, let it be said, the least restrained and reserved circles in Paris, he was being educated in the last kind of school that his mother would have chosen for him. Chères amies were as common as âmes damnées, and few notable names in art and in literature came through the assay unscathed. Still, there were sets in which liaisons were looked at askance. The returned émigrés had had a terrible lesson, and the time was not yet come for them to discard their mourning, or to wipe out of memory the horrors that relatives and even parents had been flung into, during, as it seemed to them, an accursed Yesterday. Life to them was too serious—it had become so—to countenance flippant alliances, temporary though they might be.

Association with Alfred de Musset, Chopin, Victor Hugo, George Sand, Heinrich Heine, Hector Berlioz, Eugène Delacroix, Lamartine—a few only of the artistic circle—could not fail to attenuate the scruples of a highly principled young man like Liszt. There must have been something singularly attractive about him in every period of his life. The early drawings and lithographs show him slim, thin in arm and leg, with a long, oval face, omitting in kindliness those blemishes which appear in the untouched photographs of later days, and mercifully left out in the bust which Boehm modelled of him during his last visit to London, in 1886. Having heard Paganini play, he aspired to the title of the " Paganini of the Pianoforte," but did he, with his long hair and close fitting clothes, copy him in externals, greasy collar and all? It was left to

Rossini to ask him if his long black hair was his own.

Apart from his artistic side there was a physical aspect which led artists, sculptors and painters, to invite him to sit for them. It is even alleged that in the Gardens of the Tuileries the statue of the Roman, Cincinnatus, by Foyatier (1793-1863) was modelled after him. He had sat to artists so often that by 1848 he declined to sit for a sculptor on the grounds that by this time there were far too many busts of him, medallions and statuettes, not to mention caricatures, and this shows his feeling that things in this direction had been overdone.

Much sought after for his accomplishments, and coming thereby in contact with the intellectual sets in Paris, Liszt was a man of the world before he had come of age. The homage that was accorded him was that offered by those who worship the rising star, the risen demi-god. Everywhere he was a persona grata. He seems to have played upon women's emotions with as great success and certainty as he played upon the keyboard, and that is saying much.

Doubtless it was the assurance that he was not quite as others of his age that made a deep impression on him, and realizing his limitations in matters outside music—the linguistic difficulty, perhaps, among them—he took the very natural step of balancing his defects by a great, a generous bearing towards others. Quite early, and for many a year

The Débutant

to come, he took Berlioz to heart—that same Berlioz, fiery in soul and in mane, who laid the foundations of the modern orchestra.

Many were those who courted Liszt's favours, but Countess Adèle de La Prunarède was the successful candidate, and huntress-like swept him off to her retreat in Switzerland in ransom for his dalliance, and there he entered upon his noviciate.

When he returned to Paris in 1833 it was found that his literary style in French had materially benefited by the change, but the correspondence with his hostess withered away. She was on the lookout for another young abbé *in petto*.

CHAPTER III

ELOPEMENT

George Sand, dogmatizing and dominating, was to take Liszt in hand, he, perhaps, fascinated by her dressing like a man, with a preposterously tall hat—she, full of the social system of Saint Simon, which was to regenerate a stupid and indolent civilization. There was always a certain complacency about Liszt, and though he listened, and probably was bored, by the vain shoutings of George Sand's adherents, he declared in after life that he never had advocated her theories. He was not then too deeply read—his school days ended when he was fourteen—and the likelihood is that the wild talk in his set was over his head. For literature he turned to poetry—mainly Dante—and the titles of the works that he composed in after years testify to a broad outlook and a generous appreciation of the world's masterpieces.

Of the salons that opened their doors to him, that of the Countess Marie d'Agoult attracted the most brilliant people. Berlioz was an habitué, and it was he who introduced Liszt to his hostess, who

Elopement

afterwards was the mother of Liszt's three children, Blandine, Cosima and Daniel—a beautiful woman with masses of fair hair: in character "six feet of snow on twenty of lava", and cursed with many a brain-storm. She was the daughter of Viscount de Flavigny, an émigré who had fled from France to Frankfort during the French Revolution. At Frankfort he married the daughter of a rich banker, Simon Moritz Bethmann. Half of Marie's blood, therefore, was Jewish. In 1809, when she was four years of age, her father returned to France, and died when she was thirteen. Her mother, with the tribal instinct of her race, returned to her own people in Frankfort. The journey from Paris at this time took seven days, and three nights were slept at inns. The outstanding memory of this period in Marie's life was having been patted on the head by Goethe. Her surroundings were not favourable for her upbringing, and she was sent to the Convent of the Sacred Heart, which made an impression on her romantic mind, but apparently left her morals untouched. She brought her mother to Paris, and on leaving the Convent, entered the fashionable world of salons and balls, passing her unrestrained youth in this atmosphere. When she was twenty-two she married Count Charles d'Agoult, an aristocrat with influence at Court and in Society, but nearly twice her age.

With so attractive a young wife, always dressed with distinction if not extravagance, Count Charles d'Agoult found his house becoming the centre of all that was most exclusive in the Parisian world of politics, literature and art. It was her ambition to be in the forefront of each. In those days there were two ways of accomplishing this: the difficult way, by sheer force of talent: the easier, by forming an attachment to some one with influence. She chose the second, and yielded to Émile de Girardin, who owned a newspaper, *La Presse*, run on commercial lines, to the horror of Honoré de Balzac, who broke with him on this account.[1]

It was some five or six years after her marriage that Liszt fell under her spell. In that interval he had broken his heart over Caroline Saint-Criq, had his literary style elevated by Madame de La Prunarède, and had undergone experiences, suspected but discreetly unrecorded, which prepared him for his part in " La Grande Passion."

Accounts from either side, that of the Countess or of Liszt, are unstable. But it is clear that his ardour melted the " six feet of ice." What he found when he reached the lava was his own affair. There are contradictory reports as to which of the pair was the first to fly to Switzerland, but it appears accepted that in his room in his hotel in Berne he

---

[1] Girardin married Delphine Gay, "the Tenth Muse," in June 1831. Floyd, p. 72.

Elopement

found the lady's luggage in stacks. That settled any doubts.

A move was made to Geneva—not quite tactful for the pair to choose surroundings of anointed Calvinism, and for company they had to fall back upon those who took " broad views," and ultimately to be content with themselves.

At the newly founded Conservatoire Liszt gave free music lessons. Some of his reports have survived. " Marie D——, vicious method (if it deserves the name): extreme zeal: mediocre aptitude. Grimaces and contortions. Glory to God in Heaven and peace to men of good will." " Jenny G——. Lovely eyes." [The " Gloria " would have been more appropriate here].

While private lessons were providing scanty means, the hour arrived when funds came to an end. Calvinism still showed a stiff upper lip when Liszt's name was mentioned, and he was ostracized by the more strict members of the community. A fortunate acquaintance suggested a concert, which, though poorly attended, helped a little. Thereafter things went more smoothly, with the arrival, in December 1835, of a particle of human evidence of their on-goings, thus registered:

" Blandine, natural daughter of François Liszt, professor of music, aged 24 years and one month, and of Catherine Adélaïde Méran, aged 24 years [she was 30] born at Paris, both unmarried and domiciled at Geneva."

Thus Liszt, at the age of twenty-four, found himself the father of an illegitimate child, the mother being registered under an assumed name, as unmarried, and with a false age.

Parisian society went ablaze over the elopement. A titled lady and a mere musician! That was tolerable and even amusing on the stage, but "a thing of naught" in Higher Circles. Their jeunes filles were allowed to go to Opera in Italian, because Italian singers were within the pale of the Church, and, besides, the young ladies could not understand the librettos, whereas French singers were excommunicated.[1] So at least wrote the Countess in her *Souvenirs*[2] under her well-known name of Daniel Stern.

Count Charles d'Agoult took the desertion stoically. The divorce followed, and his sole comment was, "Liszt is a man of honour." The Countess's brother used the same phrase. Both hoped that Liszt would make good in the conventional fashion, but neither he nor his partner had thought of

---

[1] As for devoutness there was a violin-player in the Opera orchestra who had to earn his daily bread, but to prevent his being induced to look at scenes which were "corruptible", he played with his back to the stage.

[2] Kapp says that in her *Souvenirs, 1806-1833*, Liszt is never mentioned, but on p. 303 he makes appearance only once, as "le petit Liszt."

Elopement 23

marriage. The theories of George Sand were their explanation if not their defence.

Meanwhile, rumours had reached Switzerland that a rival had burst into the circle of pianists. It was Thalberg. Madame d'Agoult could not brook a Viennese interloper between the public and her divinity, so back to Paris was the order of the day, to find, fortunately, that the attitude of society was less stiff and censorious.

Liszt as a pianist had nothing to fear from a rival, but he disliked having to play at a concert, even for charity, with Thalberg in the same programme. It was distasteful that two artists should have to compete for " points " given to them by the audience. Whatever may be said for the undignified affair it had the good effect of bringing Liszt back to the more congenial atmosphere of Paris. There he could find grounds more relative for his " Glorias."

At the end of the year (1836) the Countess had taken herself off to Nohant, George Sand's domain in the old Province of Berry. Liszt did not join her there till the following May. Eight or ten weeks later he and the Countess went to Italy, and on Christmas Day, at Bellagio on Lake Como, a girl was born—hence Cosima. In after days Liszt said the name came from St. Cosmo, to whom he had a " devotion."

The idea of concerts in Milan occurred to Ricordi, the well-known publisher, who desired to introduce the first pianist in the world to Italian audiences.

But while Italy had cultivated to the highest degree the appreciation of singing, it had yet to understand instrumental music, particularly in the form that Liszt gave it. In spite of the curiosity about his personality the concert was a fiasco. A voice from the stalls shouted, after one of Liszt's Études, " I go to the theatre for amusement, but not for piano exercises." Other tactics had to be devised even if the people in the boxes insisted on chattering throughout the music. Hence the improvisations on themes suggested by the audience. The threadbare tunes of Bellini and Donizetti provided themes for improvisations, but the audience merrily suggested as more fitting subjects the Cathedral of Milan or the new Railway. Liszt had his revenge. He played sonatas by Beethoven, certain in Milan as earlier in Paris, that no one would detect the trick. But he felt bitter in his heart that he was acting the charlatan, though his audiences were not aware of the irony of it all.

Disastrous floods in Hungary roused him to help his fellow-countrymen who had suffered, and he went to Vienna to raise contributions to the Relief Fund by giving concerts. The result was the handsome sum of 25,000 gulden. In spite of this magnificent gesture, criticism was forthcoming in an astonishing form. The Empress of Austria wanted to hear Liszt play at a command concert, but as his reputation by now was well known through his

Elopement

liaison with Madame d'Agoult, and his intimacy with George Sand, it was decided to consult the police before so signal a favour as Royal Patronage could be granted. It was suggested that there could not be any insidious political propaganda, and moreover, Liszt was an Austrian subject. Tunes more than once have created a state of " nerves " in the Chancelleries of Europe.

The reply of the police to the inquiry was "pikant." It came by return of post, and showed that Liszt's dossier was fairly complete. It stated that he kept bad company in Paris which imperilled his character not so much politically as morally. It noted his association with George Sand and her evil works and notorious adherents. His liaison with Madame d'Agoult was mentioned, as well as the places that he had visited with her. Then came the amazing pronouncement :—

" He is particularly vain and frivolous, affecting the fantastic manners of the young Frenchmen of to-day, and apart from his value as an artist he is quite an insignificant young man."

The letter went on to call attention to the distinction of playing before the Court, and praised Liszt's generosity in connection with the floods in Hungary. The Minister of Police concluded by saying that if at a later date the question of conferring upon Liszt the rank of Imperial-Royal Chamber-Artist should arise, he would not risk giving assent to the suggestion, at any rate for the present.

All the same, Liszt did play, and though he had to wait twenty years, he was ultimately decorated by the Austrian Emperor, receiving the Cross of the Order of the Iron Crown which carried with it the patent of nobility, dated October 30th, 1858.

By January, 1839, Liszt was in Rome with the Countess and the two little girls. The Holy City was not having the best effect upon him. Its atmosphere was too " black," and revived that sombre tinge of mysticism which had been obscured by the garish opinions of George Sand and her intimates. Besides, as an artist not yet in his thirtieth year, with two young children, aged respectively four and two years, and prospects of a third, a son, as it happened, not to speak of a somewhat exacting mistress, he had to take stock of his own position and of his art.

Rest assured that the Countess, with her keen and disconcerting evaluation of character, saw his difficulties and coolly analysed them. She had given up all for his sake—honour and home—all, too, to yield to a caprice. She had been the mother of his children, and of the four years of the liaison many months had been resigned to the cares of maternity. She had sacrificed her social position for a man who, in her eyes, had not yet emerged from some chrysalis state. It was bitter enough to find herself in the shadow as a paramour, while others no better or worse than herself were tolerated in these Roman days, when men in high positions felt themselves so secured and screened by laxity in even higher places that they could snap their fingers at hints of banishment. She knew too well the seventeenth-century Guy Patin's maxim, " Vere Cardinales isti sunt carnales."

But Marie d'Agoult was a Countess in her own right by birth, and by marriage to a member of the French Nobility, and it was gall to her to find Liszt complacently accepting invitations which did not include her as well. Therein lay the hurt. No number of genuflexions could redress the scale when wounded pride was in the balance. Mentally and in all other respects on a higher plane than Liszt's, she was left to take care of her children, mewed up in an insanitary flat, awaiting the birth of her third child, while he, for whom she had forsaken position, dignity and ambition, swept in all that he coveted. Small wonder, then, that there were misunderstandings. She was proud of the homage laid at his feet, but when she came to see the emptiness of it all she revolted. Casting things up in her mind, she asked herself what Liszt was about during the early months of 1837, when she was with George

Sand at Nohant, whither he joined her nearly five months later.

Constancy and loyalty were strangers in her marriage to Charles d'Agoult: both were united in Liszt, and she expected him to give to her what he was receiving. There was no open breach as yet, but she was gradually realizing the injuries from which Liszt as " a man of honour " ought to have protected her. For him there was only one way out—to resume the rôle of " vagabond indefatigable " as Berlioz called him, but an excuse had to be found. It came by chance. France had subscribed a pitiful sum, less than 500 francs, towards the Beethoven monument in Bonn. Liszt was indignant and at once asked his sculptor-friend in Florence, Bartolini, what it would cost. The reply was 60,000 francs. Liszt guaranteed the sum, to be raised by concert-giving during a tour in Europe.

In May, Liszt's son Daniel was born, and towards the end of the year the Countess and the children were sent to Paris to be under the care of Liszt's mother.

CHAPTER IV

VAGABOND INDEFATIGABLE

The occurrences of a given period must be studied in relation to contemporary conditions. Therefore the mind has to conceive a time—in the years 1839 and 1840—when there were few railways, no telegraphs, no photographers, no press-agents in Europe generally. Musical affairs were for the most part local. The arrival of some one pre-eminent in his art did not cause the complete confusion of other plans, for no organization existed. The "star" artist was no better off than the circus proprietor who pitched his tents wherever the town authorities permitted. The musical "star" did not find every hall engaged eighteen months ahead. There was little competition: little inducement to travel. Hence it was possible for a young man in Liszt's position to find an audience wherever he chose, and a room to accommodate him. If the piano was out of tune, so much the better, we are told: it suggested ideas.

Liszt's loyal desire to help his Hungarian compatriots brought all Hungary to his feet. But while he ennobled himself by sympathy and humanity, he imperilled his character by yielding to displays which the more reserved put down as conduct appropriate to a talented charlatan. In later years he was to be burdened by an inexorable penance for this.

This visit to Vienna at the end of 1839 was not quite like that of two years before when the Minister of Police disclosed the contents of Liszt's dossier. No General returning from a triumphant campaign could have desired a greater ovation than this young man who had just passed his twenty-eighth birthday. What was called " Lisztomanie " was spreading. The world of music had seen nothing to be compared with it : even Wagner in the Bayreuth period could not compete with like enthusiasm. Such welcomes now-a-days are reserved for cinema " stars."

In Pest, Liszt was received as a national hero, and the Hungarian magnates in national costume presented him in the name of Hungary with a sword of honour. Those who did not know the significance of the ceremony cast ridicule upon the proceedings, and Liszt was led to protest in a letter to the *Revue des Deux Mondes*, writing in French, having forgotten his Hungarian, as has already been mentioned. He had to point out that the presentation was a national characteristic and a patriotic distinction. A further honour was added in the form of the Freedom of the City. The enthusiasm with which his frequent concerts were received left the funds for

Vagabond Indefatigable 31

the Beethoven monument amply secured. But the contrast between the two composers most concerned—Liszt, the means: the end, Beethoven's memory—and the manner of their lives, might give rise to many a cynical reflection.

Liszt was not allowed to pass out of the limelight into shadow and solitude. When he visited his birthplace, Raiding, there was no escape, one way or another, from the theatrical parade of gipsies with their special instruments, dances and songs. They claimed him as one of themselves. The flourish was national rather than musical.

The more critical in the musical world were agape at such ongoings. Liszt disliked them, but was powerless to stop them without giving offence. So striking a figure could not escape notice wherever he went, and he was seized upon by Hungary, in need of a national hero at the time. There were underground murmurings against Austrian rule, and the authorities may have smiled at the demonstrations as a fortunate diversion of public attention.

Meanwhile Leipzig, priding itself on being the musical centre of Europe, was on guard, and what Leipzig thought was beyond all challenge. It was here that Liszt, who had been carrying all before him, was to sustain his first defeat. The purpose of his tour seems to have been overlooked. The Leipzigers may have had in mind something about fearing "Danaos dona ferentes." We shall see later what happened in Bonn in 1845 when the Beethoven monument was inaugurated. For the present whether as composer or pianist—a man who had been making enormous sums by his recitals—he was passing into an atmosphere of jealousy. He had aroused antagonism by disregarding custom and suspending the "free list." The first concert was given on March 17, 1840. He appeared on the platform in silence, and the first number, his arrangement of the *Pastoral Symphony*, was greeted with some hisses. The recital was a fiasco. Liszt was deeply wounded, took to his bed and postponed the next concert. Schumann said it was a diplomatic illness —eine politische Krankheit.

Although Schumann and Mendelssohn were then on friendly terms with him and spent long hours by his bedside, Schumann could not refrain from writing to his Clara that he and Liszt inhabited different worlds in music. Liszt's he said was tinsel —Flitterwesen—a singular comparison, for a few days later, in another letter, he records Liszt's complaint that the nobility and aristocracy round about Leipzig dressed very dowdily. Evidently tinsel was out of fashion in these parts as much in modes as in music. Liszt's comment is significant, for whatever his own simplicity and humility in his later years, he was always attracted by handsomely dressed and beautiful women, preferably

Vagabond Indefatigable

those with titles. This was remarked of him even forty years later. Clara Wieck noted that his conversation was that of an intelligent man of the world, without ceremony, but that she soon tired of his restless vivacity.

In spite of Mendelssohn's interest if not sympathy with Liszt as an artist, the press continued hostile and the bitterest hurt came from Clara's father, because Liszt had supported her engagement to Schumann, an engagement which Friedrich Wieck had opposed, and with no small penetration. At a later date she too became irreconcilable.

The illness of Countess d'Agoult brought Liszt to Paris. She had come to terms with her family, but a section of Parisian society still declined to countenance the liaison.

From the abundant warmth of the Hungarian snow of 1839-1840, Liszt passed into the chilly spring of Leipzig, from the Tropics to the Arctic. Out of these experiences it could not have been an easy matter for him to discover the raiment in which to garb his mind. Still, during his short visit in Paris there was an event, of small import at the time, but one which ultimately was to change him in more than one sense into a man of a very different cloth.

Undaunted by the Leipzig set-back he was planning fresh realms to conquer when a young man presented himself with a letter of introduction from

Schlesinger, a music publisher in Paris. Liszt, living in comfort if not luxury, must have received many a begging letter, many an impecunious compatriot stranded in Paris. This visitor could speak German only, a language which Liszt was yet to learn, while Liszt in French was unable to understand what his half-starved caller wanted. The interview collapsed. The visitor, noting the surroundings, the signs of well-being that were not his, and with an ache in his heart, turned abruptly and left the room. His name was Richard Wagner.

About this time Liszt paid several visits to London, in the summer 1840 and again in the winter, returning in the following summer. His two recitals in June were received with enthusiasm, shortly after his appearance at a concert of the Philharmonic Society, when he played, as "Mr. Franz Liszt," Weber's *Concertstück*. For his service, he was presented with "a piece of plate, valued at forty guineas." In those days the Society did not always pay its "stars" in cash: gifts of plate or jewelry were quite frequently made. In the winter he played before Queen Victoria at Windsor, and left England in February.

Evidently all had gone well, so London saw him again in the summer of 1841. On this occasion, however, the irrepressible Countess insisted on accompanying him, but the tour brought disaster to his impresario, and had to be ended abruptly.

It is not necessary to go far out of the way for an explanation. The presence of the Countess was sufficient. Although Prince Albert had been Consort for just about eighteen months, his influence over English society was making itself felt. For any success in music the patronage of the aristocracy was essential: it was withheld, and gossip did the rest. Two houses only were open to him, those of Lady Blessington and Count d'Orsay. That sums up the situation.

Liszt's audiences seem to have swung between two extremes: the pæans of Hungary—the silence of Leipzig: the enthusiasm of London in one year, to be followed a twelve-month later by indifference. Berlin was to repeat this, as will shortly be seen. It was as if these receptions were an inversion of the Countess's character, six feet of snow on twenty of lava—but now by an ironic perversion of thermodynamics, six feet of lava on twenty of snow.

The humiliation sank deep, but Liszt was experiencing what the Countess had felt in Rome when she was neglected. Coming after the reconciliation with her family and a better understanding on all sides, it was a blow to them both. They were sharing misfortune, and this was bringing them together.

At a short distance from Bonn on the Rhine are a pair of small islands, of which one, Nonnenwerth, with a disused convent, took Liszt's fancy. Here, he felt, he might find a haven for the Countess and their family. There was something plausible in his announcement to her that he had taken a lease of the island, with protests that there yet might be years of peace before them, forgetting that they had just left five stormy years behind them, and no assurance that they would not continue. However, the family arrived at the island and spent three summers there.

Cologne was only a little way off, and during excursions in the neighbourhood Liszt heard that a movement was on foot to ask for subscriptions in order to complete the building of the Cathedral. This had been begun some fifteen years before (1824) but primarily to preserve it as it then stood. When Liszt suggested that he might help by giving a concert the idea was welcomed with enthusiasm, and he supplemented the receipts with a donation.

At all times throughout his life Liszt gave freely. Splendidly responsive as was the public whenever he gave a concert in a good cause, he in turn was munificent, and there was none more than he who recognized that his was a gift to be used in the service of man, and who kept ever before him the phrase that he had coined, " Génie oblige." The pity is that for all his bountifulness there was not more self-restraint on the part of his audiences. He himself felt this. He would have been happier with his piano. But

Vagabond Indefatigable

curiosity to see, if not to listen to him, became infectious. It was as if fashion had decided that it was the correct thing to stare at him. Once the fever started it spread like an epidemic, and he who excused many an excess of his own was powerless to check it. The opportunity was too good to be lost. So it happened that in Cologne and in the little village of Rolandseck, opposite Nonnenwerth, there was a sort of pageant. It set out from Cologne with chorus and band, flowers and streamers, to honour Liszt in his island and thank him for his generosity. He was greeted by salvos from guns as if he had been a great soldier—with flag-waving and delirium. Well, he had experienced something of the kind in Hungary—there, as a belted swordsman—here, somehow connected with artillery.

The ovation was too much for him. He had not the strength of purpose to make a breach by retiring for a year or two, for with foresight he was secure financially for the rest of his life. He had only to open his piano and the money flowed in. The old blood stirred in this man little over thirty years of age: he must be in the lime-light again—vagabond indefatigable—on another concert-tour: or was it an excuse to get away from his Countess?

After the extravagances on the Rhine Liszt was all aglow for further demonstrations. These were not lacking. Initiation as a free-mason at Frankfort: a meeting with Spohr in Cassel: a students' "rag" with much smashing of glasses and windows at Bonn : a decoration (Falken-Orden) and diamond ring at Weimar : duet-playing in Leipzig with Clara, now Schumann's wife : but these were but mild preludes to the incredible visit to Berlin. It was at Leipzig that Clara finally made up her mind that Liszt, with his "chaos of dissonances" made her shudder, and after his playing on December 15, 1841, Beethoven's *E Flat Concerto* and the performance of his chorus for male voices, *Was ist der Deutschen Vaterland*, Liszt and all his works were proscribed.

He was to have his revenge before the month was up, and yet not quite a revenge, for the happenings must have rejoiced the hearts of many of the dull Leipzig musicians, with head-shakings and finger-waggings, with many a "I told you so!"

Still, for all that did occur in Berlin, with Liszt acquiescent, he accomplished an amazing feat. Thus :

Length of stay in Berlin		10 weeks
Number of public concerts	12	
Number of concerts for charity	9	21 concerts
Number of works performed of which 50 were given from memory.	80	
Number of private concerts, not stated.		

Vagabond Indefatigable 39

With this record it cannot be said that Liszt mis-spent his time. His industry must be set against the folly of the Berliners. The academic honours that were showered upon him, culminating with the Order, "Pour le Mérite" bestowed by Frederick William IV, were due as much to his broad sympathies as to his art. There was something indecent in the manner in which the people of Berlin during these ten weeks flung aside all self-control and gave themselves up to an orgy of "Lisztomanie." From the ceremonies of the Court, the Assemblies of the University and learned Societies, down to the vulgar scrambles for anything that Liszt had touched, there was an absence of dignity which the wiser citizens deplored. It was unheard of that the Order of Merit, purely military in its restrictions, should have been conferred upon a mere pianist. Even Mendelssohn turned his back in disgust, and the breach between the two was never healed.

There were some who felt shame that their city should have presented so ludicrous a spectacle to the world, and the caricaturists, dramatists and satirists saw their opportunity and held it fast.

How did Liszt take it all? By now he was so accustomed to audiences committing unthinkable acts in their delirious applause that the homage may have appeared to him quite a normal affair. He does not seem to have been conscious of the harm that it was doing to himself, or to have taken any steps to put an end to an incredible state of mind on the part of his admirers.[1] On the contrary he "played up." But when he paid his next visit to Berlin, at the beginning of 1843, in spite of the welcome from the Court and the bestowal of the gold medal for Art and Science, the people, only too mindful of the indiscretions of the preceding year, and blushing for the shamelessness of their conduct, avoided the concerts and ignored the man.

He "played up" at the end of the earlier period. In order to assist at his departure for Russia, the University suspended its sittings for the day. Liszt was received as if he were a crowned head. He set out in a carriage drawn by six white horses, with beside him the President of the Students' Corps in full uniform. Thirty carriages drawn by four horses (the distinction is worthy of note) followed, and a cavalcade of mounted students wearing their special colours acted as escort. After this, as it were, official convoy, there came a hundred private carriages, decorated for the occasion. Even the Court came to town to take part in the ceremony, and the business was made a public event. When it was over the people began to realize what fools they had made of themselves.

If his audiences in Russia and elsewhere showed

[1] See p. 49 for Belloni's tactics and Heine's charges.

Vagabond Indefatigable

more restraint, he was not disposed to tone down his love for display, and startled the Court by appearing with his coat covered with stars and decorations. Nevertheless there was the same enthusiasm, the same lavishness on the part of his audiences and on Liszt's, and he seems to have lost all idea of proportion in the lengths to which he went. Whether it was for charity or for private entertainments, the sums that passed through his hands must have been enormous. The crowning act of folly was his travelling in a caravan, probably like that of the proprietor of a circus—with dining-room, bedroom and kitchen all in one: with horses and a body-servant to shave him and decide which of his three hundred and sixty neckties he was to wear. Was ever ring-master better found? An eye-witness who was Liszt's host in Belgium, describes, not the caravan, but the crowd who escorted him from town to town in his triumphal progress, and among the people were women in men's attire. The same informant[1] spoke of the outbreak of frenzy that impelled people to cut snippets from his coat, to drag his carriage through the streets, to tear his gloves from him and to forget themselves in hysterics.

We do not know if he entered Dresden in the caravan. Had it been later in Munich we can well

[1] Kapp says, p. 166, "Selbst Frauen, die sich als Männer verkleideten, um ihm zu folgen," quoting as his authority the *Memoirs* of Charles Dubois of Liège, 1841-42, who was his host.

understand the joy it would have created in the heart of Wagner's patron, Ludwig the Second, whose love for the spectacular and outré was notorious. As it was, in Dresden Wagner's *Rienzi* was being staged, and Liszt, ever curious about new works and their composers, went to hear it. During an interval he found his way to the dressing-room of the tenor, and there met Wagner for the second time. A word or two of congratulations and then Wagner espied a painted and bejewelled woman with insolent eyes: he turned and fled. Liszt had been living with the lady for some weeks, without regard for the Countess or even for his children, and the lady's name was Lola Montez.

With Lola, as with others, known and unknown, it was *Da Capo al Segno*. He tired of her. There was something farcical and at the same time ignoble in this great artist having to bribe the hall-porter to smuggle him and his luggage out of his hotel and lock the lady in her room till he got clear away. The lady, furious at being imprisoned for twelve hours, smashed everything in the room. But this was after adventures in Paris and elsewhere. Later on she appeared with Liszt, à la suite, as it were, at the Beethoven Festival at Bonn in 1845. After Liszt had disposed of her in the manner just described, she flew to the open arms of Ludwig the First of Bavaria, and with the perfect nonchalance with which ladies of her disposition change their gear, offered Liszt the highest decoration that Bavaria could bestow.

A couple of decades later the Bavarian newspapers commented with some point upon another Lola Montez—the Second—who was battening upon the grandson of Ludwig the First, and the dubious nickname was conferred upon Richard Wagner. Thus by a twist of Fortune, ever cynical in these matters, Lola came round full circle, in name at least. There must have been many a regret in Liszt's mind that he had not locked up the Second as he had the First.

Of what interest was it to him that five years after this adventure he should receive a letter from an actress, Charlotte von Oven, née von Hayn, dated May 24th, 1849, telling him that Lola had gone to America?

CHAPTER V

BÉATRIX—NÉLIDA

For all the artist that he was, preux chevalier sans peur et sans réproche that was claimed for him, Liszt's adventurings with a woman of the stamp of Lola Montez or with some Dame aux Camellias, put his liaison with Madame d'Agoult on the lowest level. Even in such matters there is a convention, an etiquette, a social observance. Things might have been understood had the Montez been a Countess: by all the unwritten rules only a Countess, or someone higher, could displace a Countess: an Amurath by an Amurath. By this incredibly false step Liszt alienated, degraded his mistress, and cast a shadow over his children, although they had been legitimated through the offices of the Empress of Austria, Liszt being an Austrian subject. Despite the elasticity of the social code, there was at least some respect due to the mother of his children, now that the irregular union had been recognized and condoned, although from the point of view of her family he had not proved himself " a man of honour." Later on, however, he made good the balance by replacing one Countess, his chère amie, by another, with the title of Princess, who was to haunt him as his âme damnée.

About this time a shrewd observer of the Human Comedy, himself a comedian, was all eyes and ears. An intimate of George Sand's, but never trespassing beyond the line of friendship, Honoré de Balzac had heard from his top-hatted friend the story of Liszt and the Countess. Balzac could not keep his mind off character, whether good or bad. He knew the Countess, described by him as " an interesting type of woman-artist, gifted with great intelligence and startling beauty ". On hearing her story he concocted a pallid romance and called it *Béatrix*, the heroine being, in his own words, " trop bien Madame d'Agoult." Its composition was spread over five years, worked out more fitfully than in those heat-waves of creation when, supported by black coffee, he wrote daily for sixteen hours. *Béatrix* was meant to be romantic, but to quote the opinion of one of his most recent critics, André Le Breton, " When Balzac tries to be poetic he is execrable," and the story is dull. With his customary fondness for the resonance of aristocratic names, the heroine is Mademoiselle Béatrix Maximilienne Rose de Casteran afterwards the Marquise de Rochfide. She had an " amour musical " with one Conti (untitled) and was pursued by young Calyste du Guénic, one of Balzac's many instances of a young man falling in love with a woman older than himself, the pre-eminent case being his own—his liaison with Madame de Berny. (When it began he was under twenty-five, and she was over forty. Liszt, it will be remembered, was six years younger than the Countess d'Agoult.) Calyste eventually marries, but is not cured of his infatuation, and deserts his wife. The feeble dénouement comes about with reconciliation, chiefly through the offices of a celebrated Parisian doctor, who is mentioned openly and undisguised—Dommanget—" médecin-accoucheur." It was he among others who supplied Balzac with many pathological details in his novels. He seems to have been alive when *Béatrix* was published. This was in 1844, the year in which Liszt and Madame d'Agoult parted. Balzac's portrait was not uncomplimentary, but he did not conceal his dislike for her, remarking that " she was a dreadful creature of whom Liszt was glad to be rid." But perhaps the aristocrat in her disdained the man who, great as he was, affected the " particule *de* ", which he got from his father without any claims to use it, and boasted kinship with Henry the Fourth's Balzac d'Entraigues.

A point seems to have been missed by those French critics who have so fully analysed Balzac's works, for while in *Béatrix* George Sand, under the name of Mademoiselle des Touches, and others have been identified, Conti, the lover, bears no resemblance to Liszt, or indeed to any musician of the period.

When the novel was published the Countess was

Béatrix—Nélida

furious. Balzac had exasperated her, but she could ill compete with so fluent a master, so minute a dissecter of character. She had to admit that she was fairly accurately described in the book, and urged Liszt to call Balzac out. But Liszt by this time had no mind to quarrel with a friend about a lady with whom he was about to break off relations, if he had not actually done so. Balzac, again, was no fire-eater for all his rhodomontades : he had been locked up for his refusal to enlist in the National Guard, and was the last person to stand up in a duel. Probably he was one of the few writers of his time who had not crossed a rapier, or looked down the barrel of a pistol in some affair of honour.

The Countess retorted in a strange fashion. Two years later, under her nom de plume, Daniel Stern, she laid bare her relations with Liszt in a vapid tale called *Nélida*. She herself was the heroine, Mademoiselle Nélida de Thieullaye, married to the Comte Timoléon de Kervaëns (she had caught the trick of high-sounding names from Balzac), the hero Liszt, otherwise Guermann Régnier, a painter. Balzac does not appear to have been used as a character, but he had already taken her measure and disarmed her in a flash.

France, with her maîtres d'armes has never been in lack of maîtres de mots. If ever Balzac had more than a word to say to her, it was merely a form of galanterie d'epiderme to pass the time.

CHAPTER VI

THE BEETHOVEN MONUMENT

It would be misleading to say that Liszt's fantastics were accepted or tolerated by his friends. In Berlin Mendelssohn, as we have seen, silently rebuked, then dropped him. Schumann in spite of ardent professions was ill-tempered, and looked upon Liszt as something of a showman. Heine was more blunt. Criticizing two concerts given by Liszt, which brought in 12,000 francs each, he called them a "Schwindel," a double-edged word which might mean obtaining money by a trick, or the more mild "humbug".[1]

Liszt protested and called upon Heine. There was a hot argument, but Heine, far from withdrawing a syllable, made things worse by adding to his criticism an assertion that the press had been

[1] This word "Schwindel" was used by Brahms of Liszt's *Christus* when performed in Vienna at Christmas—1876 (see Kapp, 469). "Fabulously tedious, silly and absurd", were his epithets. But somewhere we have heard these very words applied to one of Brahms' own works. "Schwindel" seems to have been bestowed impartially upon Wagner's work as well. Writing to Princess Sayn-Wittgenstein from Bayreuth in March, 1877, Liszt quotes a conversation with Princess Metternich, giving her words in German, "I don't bother about the Wagner-Schwindel, but the German Schwindel which is connected with it is repugnant to me."

The Beethoven Monument

bribed and the ovations bought. It was "sheer madness, unheard of in the annals of enthusiasm."[1]

It would seem that at the root the opposition to Liszt as a musician was on all fours with much of the opposition to Wagner. It lay as much with the man as with his music. Even in those days there was something left in men disdainful of the ad captandum devices of externals, of parades and shows which ill accorded with the dignity of the art. This self-consciousness found its outlet in extravagances which not a few contemporaries regarded with scant favour. Artists were prone to arrogate to themselves the right to defy the current code of manners and draft their own, and this was the considered opinion of men who lived in the same milieu, who were keenly alive to displays that were artificial, whose vision penetrated beneath the richly or grotesquely decorated shell, to find a kernel either withered and shrunken, or less in keeping with an elaborate and flamboyant exterior.

If Liszt at this time (1845) had shown a little more strength of character, which, backed by another person, was on stray occasions to break through his complacency for the sake of peace, he might have kept in mind the circumstances attending his first appearance in Leipzig, and made concessions. But there was too much to be said against

[1] Heine stated that Liszt's secretary, Belloni, sent in a bill for "ovation expenses, wreaths, bouquets, etc.," to the tenor, Rubini, who had been on tour with Liszt.

him. Envious of his unsurpassable mastery of the keyboard, jealous of the golden harvest of his fingers, scornful of his disregard for strictly scholastic methods, the Kapellmeisterei of Leipzig and of Saxony viewed with misgivings the advent of this musical revolutionary. And the caravan-business was not forgotten—the lion in a cage whose bars were of pure gold.

It was not with the utmost goodwill in the world that the Committee, entrusted with the celebrations connected with the inauguration of the Beethoven monument at Bonn, accepted the services of this upstart, not yet thirty-four years of age. Beethoven they knew something about: they were proud that he had been born among them: although they were less proud that he had preferred Vienna as his abiding-place, an Austrian in sympathy, like Haydn, Mozart and Schubert, Flemish by descent, not even Saxon like Handel and Bach, and behold! his monument erected, not by Saxon, Fleming, or Austrian, but by the efforts of a comparatively young man from Hungary. Where, indeed, was Hungary?

Yet in their hearts the people of Bonn had to recognize that this Liszt was no mere mechanic. His technique was to give them many a sleepless night, with fingers playing over the dumb bed-covers in vain emulation of this magician. These shakes, these arpeggios, these thundering octaves

The Beethoven Monument 51

—all within reach, but so distant in their effect! Something he had that they could vie with only in dreams: but there it was, to their discomfiture, and they cherished resentment.

However laudable his desire to see the monument at Bonn worthy of Beethoven, and however generous his contribution to the fund, it was not as a persona grata that Liszt was present. To have left him out of the number of guests would have been scandalous. The Committee had been none too tactful in rejecting his offer of 60,000 francs and a marble statue by Bartolini. A German sculptor was preferred, so Liszt withdrew his offer and contributed 10,000 francs instead. The Committee chose a mediocre bronze by someone else. Then it was found that the hall in which the celebrations were to take place was too small, and once more Liszt put his hand in his pocket, and in ten days a temporary structure befitting the occasion was erected at his expense.

With blazing indiscretion Liszt included Lola Montez in his party. This did not help to relieve the general feeling of tension. The Celebrations do not appear to have been organized very efficiently. Liszt's special work on the programmes was his *Festival Cantata*, to be performed on the third day. It was rendered half-heartedly, but just as it finished, the King of Saxony, for whom everybody had been waiting, entered the hall, and Liszt repeated the Cantata, this time with brilliancy.

Temper was the prevailing note at the final banquet. According to Moscheles who was present, Liszt made an unfortunate speech when the toasts came round, and excited to anger the representatives of France by omitting all reference to that country. This may, or may not have been designed: Paris had contributed only 424 francs, 90 centimes to the fund. Although he declared that he had made his home in France for years, and that nothing was further from his mind than to slight a country that was dear to him, the Frenchmen present were not appeased, and recriminations and quarrels became so violent that the ladies left the room in terror. There was general uproar and the function was so demoralized that the question arose whether the concluding concert should take place.

Liszt was disgusted that the inauguration should have been seized as the opportunity for the display of partisanship, due to a large extent to his faux pas, and felt that the memory of Beethoven should have been held far above all personal differences. Very wisely he declined the proposal of the town to name a street after him. To him it had been a pride to shoulder generously his part in the memorial, but it was soiled by the ignoble squabble into which the festival had degenerated.

The sequel is interesting. When the Centenary of Beethoven's birth was celebrated in October, 1870, Liszt was not invited to take part, and his rival

The Beethoven Monument

and detractor, Hiller, was given the principal post. This may have been due to Liszt's attitude during the Franco-Prussian War (he had a great admiration for Napoleon III), but more likely to the Bonn people regarding him, with the earlier proceedings in mind, as a stormy petrel.

The experiences in Bonn in 1845 went some way to strengthen his conviction that he ought to retire from public life with its enmities and jealousies. This may have had something to do with his proposal of marriage to Countess Valentine Cassiat, a niece of the poet Lamartine. The lady could not make up her mind, but her uncle, knowing perhaps too much of Liszt's past history, his fickleness and restlessness, settled the matter for her, deciding that it would be unwise to entrust his niece to a man who was unlikely ever to accommodate himself to home life. It may have been in Liszt's mind that through this marriage might be found a wholehearted reason for anchorage at last, and for leading a regular existence devoted entirely to composition. But there were obstacles—the Countess d'Agoult—the children—possibly other dependents. Lamartine decided that the risk was too great. For once a poet was beneath the clouds.

If the refusal did not touch Liszt deeply, it had one immeasurably good effect, for it led him to Weimar, a town to be associated with his name, and to provide the nearest semblance of a home that at any time he was likely to possess. It was here, indeed, in surroundings consecrated by memories of Goethe and Schiller, Herder and Wieland, that he was to advance the cause of the great masters, to discover a field for opera, and to seek out and encourage talent.

But before settling down he planned a tour that was to be final—one which, had he foreseen the consequences, he well might have hesitated to undertake. Eastern Europe was to be the scene, and Silesia, Rumania and Turkey were visited, till in September, 1847, in Elizabethgrad, he gave his last public recital. Henceforth he was to play in public only for charity or to raise funds for some endowment.

This tour, however, was to have a far-reaching effect, for in Kiev, in February, 1847, he met the lady who bound up his destiny with hers. She was Princess Carolyne Sayn-Wittgenstein.

CHAPTER VII

ENTER THE PRINCESS

In an attempt to examine the surroundings and complicated lives of fantastical beings who have jostled one another and trapesed upon the musical stage, it is not easy to reconcile antagonistic professions. Devoutness, hand in glove with a disregard for moral codes, no matter were they the approved codes of the hour, had more than a strain of insincerity : it was almost grotesque.

In his art and in his strivings there was something noble and monumental about Liszt : but in a worldly sense he had climbed to the sacrosanct pillar of some Simon Stylites by the ladder afforded by loose unions, temporary entanglements, impenitent liaisons. If, as he said, " génie oblige," more than " noblesse oblige," he was demanding for himself a special consideration which he rigorously withheld in the case of his own daughter, and yet there was as much " génie " in her as there was in him.

Or was it that the suggestion of his dying father that he was destined to fall a prey to the domination of women, had entered so fatally into his thoughts

Liszt, Wagner, and the Princess

that he yielded only too easily? There was a readiness, almost an indelicate haste, with which he allowed himself to be won by the lady who, for the rest of his life was to be the nether millstone —we shall see presently who was the upper millstone.

The Thirteenth of February was a date to be well remembered by two persons who were afterwards to find themselves in close, though not always harmonious, relationship with a third. It was on this date that Liszt, when giving a charity concert —in his admirable way—was caught by the blazing eye of the Princess Carolyne Sayn-Wittgenstein, found his destiny, and determined her own. It was on a Thirteenth of February that Richard Wagner died, the man to whom in after years both were to forfeit peace of mind and worldly goods.

Carolyne was the only child of a Polish nobleman, Peter von Iwanowsky and Pauline von Podoska, his wife. She was born in February 8th, 1819, at Monasterzyska in the Province of Kiev. On May 7th, 1836, she married Prince Nikolaus Sayn-Wittgenstein, a handsome but undistinguished young man, and on February 9th, 1837, she presented him with a daughter, Marie. (These dates are given merely to complete the family chronology at this time.)

Shortly after the birth of her daughter she left her husband for her estate, Woronince, a large property between Kiev and Odessa. Here, before

Enter the Princess

she was twenty, she had on her hands the management of her widespread inheritance, and the upbringing of her child, who left her only on her marriage with Prince Constantin Hohenlohe-Schillingsfürst. A capable young woman, this, with her open air life, her daring in the saddle, her black cigars—let us hope not the knout—and all the advantages of her social position and wealth. To her husband she did not return, but found consolation in literature and philosophy : well educated to begin with, but too much inclined to pose as a précieuse, and ultimately as a theologian, with untoward results.

While in Kiev, early in the year 1847, she went to a charity concert given by Liszt, and paid 100 roubles for her ticket. Liszt sent his secretary, Belloni, to ask if he might come and play to her. This could not be arranged, as she was then stopping at an hotel. He had to be content with sending her a note of thanks. Shortly afterwards she was deeply moved by hearing in a church a composition of Liszt's, and she recognized in him a great artist with a future. It is not the case, however, that it was she who induced him to give up his appearances in public as a " virtuoso." That step, as we have seen, was in his mind before he met the Princess.

An invitation to Woronince arrived in due course, and ultimately in February, 1848, about the time of Marie's eleventh birthday the issue was placed beyond all doubt. These past months had seen the fulfilment of the Princess's aims. She had cast her radiance over Liszt and the harvest of compositions was rich: she had before her eyes the tribute that she imagined was to be paid to him as a great composer, happily ignorant of the worm i' the bud that was to poison her hopes.

It was a time of great serenity to Liszt: he was working as he desired, cloistered, as he may have thought, with a woman far above him in rank, but all the world to him: enjoying at last the goodly labour and companionable understanding that are beyond all price.

But it could not last. The fulminating flashes of the Church against the irregular union came as a warning. The lightning threat against those who violate the laws of Holy Church was but a prelude to the sullen, distant rumblings of the guns of 'Forty-eight all over Europe. From one or other neither was proof nor immune.

If the Princess and Liszt had been as unscrupulous in their devotions as they were in their morals, they might have attitudinized in face of the lightning. But she was a Russian subject, with property in Russia, hide-bound by restrictions which had been built up by superstition, by autocratic assumption of power, and as she saw the gathering clouds, she with her instinct for business got rid of her property, and made ready to get away. Divorce was out of

Enter the Princess

the question. It was regarded as stupid when morganatic marriages—with the great Catherine herself to call the tune—were tolerated with an insolence and heedlessness that all the Metropolitans and Holy Synods of Orthodox Russia had to look on with eyes half closed. Her faith, however, and Liszt's, was Latin. But the foot had to be put down somewhere, and the Princess and her case were crushed beneath the heel.

The guns of Revolutions were becoming too eloquent, and in the huddle Russia paled. Warnings in those days were communicated by courier, and orders were given that all main roads out of Russia were to be closed. But the Princess, whose presence of mind was ready for an emergency, passed over the frontier in her travelling carriage, with her child, her servants and her baggage just before the high gates clanged. She was out of Russian toils—for a little : then to join Liszt in Weimar.

At first the little capital was kind to the pair. The young Grand Duke, Karl Alexander, conscious of the benediction which Goethe and Schiller had conferred upon his tiny Principality, hoped that his capital would become the centre of artistic life in Germany. With Liszt in his ascendancy, with Liszt as the figure-head, uncommercialized art was to be encouraged.

After a few formalities the Princess took up her

undisputed abode, with her daughter and governess, in the Altenburg, a solid mansion in the outskirts of Weimar. Liszt discreetly had rooms in the Hotel zum Erbprinz. Things were looking well on the surface. Liszt had the ear of the Court and his high endeavours were approved. No less favours could have been accorded to him as the foremost pianist of the day. This tolerance was extended towards her fellow-countrywoman by the Dowager Grand Duchess, Maria Paulowna, sister of The Tzar Nikolaus I, who received her in spite of her peculiar relations with Liszt.

What occupied the Princess's mind at the outset was the question of divorce, for two rather stiff obstacles had to be surmounted. The Tzar as head of the Russian Church had authority over her, spiritually as well as temporarily, and it lay with him to veto the proceedings although she and Liszt were not members of the Orthodox Church. The Vatican, too, had a word in the matter, for they were strict adherents, a state of mind difficult to reconcile with the lax ties that held them together. Even if Liszt's life had been wholly blameless and free from earlier entanglements, there was nothing to justify the Princess's desertion of her husband or to palliate the consequences.

It is singular that a " bondieusarde " as she was, attached to all the outer symbols of her cult, steeped in casuistry to vindicate the ambiguousness of her

Enter the Princess

position, should have been vain enough to have thought that her rank would effect a speedy deliverance. The intervention of the Dowager Grand Duchess was of no avail : on the contrary it brought matters to a head unpleasantly, for the Princess was ordered to return to Russia. This she refused to do, knowing full well that once across the frontier it would be impossible to return to Weimar, and this would mean separation from her daughter. In consequence of her disregard of the Tzar's commands her Russian property was sequestrated, and settlements made on her daughter. She was an exile, in worse plight than an émigrée.

At this point, whether out of sympathy or in defiance, Liszt threw decorum to the winds, left his hotel, and took up his abode in the Altenburg with the Princess. The result of this step was easy to forecast. The Court had been lenient enough in ignoring the true state of affairs : but Liszt had gone too far. The Princess's name was struck off the roll of those who had the entrée : Liszt's invitations continued to be sent to his hotel, as though his residing at the Altenburg was not officially recognized, and later, during some public celebrations, the pair were cut dead.

The lady had put herself in a false position : it was her own choice, but little charity was shown her. Like the Countess d'Agoult she had sacrificed everything for Liszt : her country, her social position, her property. She had cared for Liszt's mother and his children: she had looked after his health. At every point he was indebted to her, except in his art, for she was not musical in his sense of the word. She acted as hostess to his friends, and often must have been worn out with their artistic theories and downright bad manners. When she first met Liszt it was her ambition to see him take his place as a great composer—perhaps the greatest of his contemporaries, but she was not sufficiently informed to realize the difficulties that beset the path of the pioneer in music. In later years her ambition took quite another turn, but in the Weimar days, though he was indebted to her for guidance and advice, for her help in collaboration, he was not giving himself out to her as he was to others, always cloistered as he was in some nook or corner of his nature.

It is difficult to understand what Liszt saw in her. Outwardly she was not attractive, dark in hair and complexion, almost Jewish in profile, with eyes described by him as those of a griffin. But she must have had personality and great ability. Apart from his work of reform and in the opera-house she dominated him. Little that he did in Weimar was allowed to escape her censorious eye. Even his correspondence had to be reviewed by her. The few moments of privacy were those afforded in his short journeys outside Weimar, les petites fugues

Enter the Princess

clandestines—as a recent biographer phrased them—and even then she demanded a daily bulletin, somewhat exhausting in its religiosity and protests of undying love. Liszt could feel the strain. Writing to a friend some years later (1855) about the Princess's visit to Berlin with her daughter, and making the round of museums and picture-galleries, he said, "That will be more valuable than walks in our parks or sterile correspondence." But his letters from this date, July 15, 1855 to the end of the month cover twenty pages of print!

Shortly before settling in Weimar in 1848 Liszt met Wagner for the third time, in an hotel in Dresden. A few months later Wagner visited Liszt in Weimar and explained his financial troubles. Scarcely had the voluminous correspondence begun than money matters intruded and persisted until Liszt broke with Wagner about eighteen years after. Wagner was anxious that *Tannhäuser* should be performed at Weimar, and Liszt saw the opportunity of giving it as a new German opera on the occasion of the Dowager Grand Duchess's birthday, French and Italian operas hitherto having had the preference. *Tannhäuser* was duly performed on February 16, 1849, but Liszt had conducted the Overture three months before. The performance, so to speak, was the tocsin of a feud, which, incredible as it is to us nowadays, was to divide the musical world into two bitterly opposed camps.

We get a little insight into the considered musical opinions of this period in the *Letters of a Leipzig Cantor*, Moritz Hauptmann, who wrote to Spohr after a performance of *Tannhäuser* that it was "utterly hateful, inconceivably clumsy, long and tiresome. . . . I thoroughly distrust a composer who is author of his own libretto." According to him Wagner was too much of a dilettante, straining after vulgar effect.

It is difficult to point to one single element about Liszt which should have inflamed his opponents. Much of the airs that he had given himself at one time—that Berlin circus!—his liaisons, his long absences from his children, his desertion of their mother—these may have accounted for a good deal, but not for all the flood of abuse. He was coming in contact with musicians like Schumann and Mendelssohn, whose mode of life was quite as inoffensive as their music.

It may have been his phenomenal brilliance in technique: Moritz Hauptmann likened it to pistol-shooting: it may have been the exuberance and extravagance of his pot-pourris. Probably it was a combination of envy of the musician with contempt for the man who had in their eyes too much of the big drum and spangles in his music.

In Leipzig the conservative party in music, allied with the Conservatoire, was grossly unfair. There was Liszt's championship of Wagner and Berlioz, to be sure, but there was his championship of Schumann as well, and many others of the Gewandhaus school of thought. If his detractors had studied his programmes they would have admitted that he was supremely impartial. But the history of music would be somewhat barren reading were it shorn of its " episodes."

By the time he had reached his fortieth year Liszt had completed four or five Symphonic Poems, with more sketched, and though the audiences might greet his *Mazeppa* with catcalls, he was splendid in his indifference, and held on his course. Susceptible as he might be to crinoline influence, he refused to be diverted from the policy which he had planned. It was only in December, 1858, after the organized opposition to the *Barber of Bagdad*, the opera by his friend Peter Cornelius, that he resolved never again to conduct opera. The outburst was not an attack upon the opera but on Liszt himself, and was due to the disloyalty of Dingelstedt, the manager, who had no sympathy with Liszt's reforms.

To discover a parallel to the opposition of Leipzig we have to go back to the close of the Eighteenth Century, when Grétry, Cherubini and others issued their manifesto, protesting that " Harmony to-day is complicated to the last degree, singers and instruments have gone beyond their natural compass. The rapidity of execution makes our music inappreciable by the ear. One step more will plunge us into chaos."

In much the same strain was the manifesto signed by Brahms, Joachim, B. Scholz and a name now forgotten, against the evolutionary school of composition. In Joachim's case the injury was the deeper, for he wrote to Liszt recanting all that he had learned from the man who gave him an early, if not his very first, engagement: who obtained for him an admirable appointment in Hanover: who encouraged and appreciated him long before he had won his public. Joachim bore such unending grudge against Liszt that when he was at the head of the Hochschule in Berlin, he refused admittance to a pupil of Liszt's unless he repudiated Liszt's doctrines. In association with Brahms he exercised an evil influence over British Music, the whole story of which has yet to be told. With Schumann things were somewhat different. Liszt had known him through his music for years before he met him face to face, but when the meeting did take place Schumann was under two influences: one, Clara Wieck, his betrothed and ultimately his wife, the other, a spicule of bone in his skull which was pressing upon his brain. A dull, morose dog: irresponsive when Liszt with all his magnanimity performed his *Genoveva* and his *Manfred*, to be thanked with a churlish growl. They were not so pretty to one another in those days. Schumann was touchy, and took the feeblest jokes as personal affronts. It called for all the goodwill in the world to disregard his fits of ill-humour.

Enter the Princess

Schumann lumbered and blundered with the baton. Whatever else he was, Liszt was all for efficiency in this sphere. So the controversy went on till Moritz Hauptmann flung his bomb at . . . Bach! He said that the *B Minor Mass* "was neutralized by long stretches of that dreary workmanship peculiar to him, especially in the long-drawn, never-ending solos. . . . Why did Bach write it? Question unsolved."

No! He was not referring to *Tannhäuser* or *Lohengrin*. What would he have said to *The Ring*?

It is not possible to review the situation from year to year. The Weimar stage is crowded with personages loyal and steadfast, with poor beings greedy of help, ready with slander, forgetful of benefits. The smallness of the quarrels is contemptible, but Liszt held his head erect. Beyond these differences, pitiful as we can now regard them, there was spite, and the spite of a woman, Clara Wieck.

These sallies have their historical value, for all the parties concerned are now in their well-hewn niches. But it was not quite a simple matter then, when Clara would have loved to rend the hair and the hateful cap of Carolyne, and the pair of them, for all their professions of friendship, would have been glad to scratch, metaphorically, one another's cheeks.

CHAPTER VIII

SCHWÄRMEREI

The German language contains a word which cannot be translated into English. It is the word "Schwärmerei." To render it in English equal to one of those dodekasyllabics in which Wagner entangled the minds of his readers would affront the language of Shakespeare and the Bible, and we should invade the domain of the chemists who rejoice in strings of compound words and formulae.

But Schwärmerei seems to have been good for the souls of Franz Liszt and Richard Wagner, and under its untranslatable name we may assess in our own way the preposterous jargon of affection in which the one addressed the other.

When Wagner wrote that letter dated June 23, 1848, beginning, "You told me lately that you had closed your piano for some time, and I presume that for the present you have turned banker," he struck the note upon which the friendship was to be founded. He wanted to "hypothecate" his scores. Evidently he had been in touch with his "most excellent friend" before this on the subject of the exchequer,

Schwärmerei

though no letters confirming this have been included in the *Briefwechsel*. We saw the barren meeting in Paris. Neither understood the language of the other, but it is likely that Liszt, had he known in what difficulties Wagner was, would not have let him go empty away. The second meeting, as we noted, was in a dressing-room in the Dresden Opera-House, when, after a hand-shake with Liszt, Wagner encountered a pair of insolent eyes, and fled. The third meeting also was in Dresden, in an hotel, where the two sealed a friendship that was meant to have been eternal.

Now, in 1848, they were drawing more closely together, and Wagner was in Weimar on a flying visit in order to discuss his finances with Liszt. As far as can be judged, he need not have reached this pass, for he was a Court official in Dresden on a fixed salary. As he was with Liszt for only a day on this occasion, the Princess had no opportunity for studying his character, if indeed she saw him then. Later in the year she was present at a performance of *Tannhäuser* in Dresden, and after Liszt's production of the Opera in Weimar on February 16, 1849, she wrote Wagner a warm letter of congratulations and thanks.

Thus began a closer intimacy which might have continued on worthy terms but for Wagner's exploit as a revolutionary in May, 1849, and his banishment from Saxony, with a warrant out for his arrest.

The police were after him for interference in matters which he, in his official position, should loyally have left alone. If not the inspirer of the Dresden Revolution, he was at least a conspirator, and with the facts or the romances which he himself supplied, he made himself look merely a coward, with not a little of the comedian in him.

His version of his part has been described in *Mein Leben*. His account has been scrutinized in regard to the facts.[1] His share was more like that of a hero of opera-bouffe. It broke down because he was meddling in affairs that he did not understand, and in this as in other adventures he had the knack of making himself supremely ridiculous. The affair was not quite as spectacular as the battle-pictures of this and an earlier period, misrepresented with their smoke and prancing steeds. He had not the wit to see that by violating his oath as a Court official he was shutting the door of every opera-house in Saxony against himself for years to come. But in this matter and indeed in most he was the last person to act on considered judgment.

We can dimly picture Liszt's dismay on hearing that a certain Herr R. Wagner, wanted by the police, was asking for him at the Hotel zum Erbprinz. Barely settled in Weimar, and resolved at all costs to secure

---

[1] See my *Richard Wagner as he Lived*, p. 112 et seq., in which measurements of buildings and distances, and a study of the range of the rifle then used by the Prussian troops, prove that *at no time* was he in the slightest danger.

goodwill for the Princess and himself, he must have felt that association with a political refugee would have a serious effect upon his position. The Princess had to be thought of. Russia had a long arm and at any time the Princess might find herself in no better plight than Wagner were she to become involved, even in theory, in an attack upon Supremacy by Divine Right. Sovereigns were still standing shoulder to shoulder. Europe might have forgotten the first Charles of England, but there had been businesses in France which resulted in the fate of Citoyen Louis Capet and his wife, l'Autrichienne. To be sure, it was only the other day that that volatile nation had swapped kings, and at this very moment events were taking place disturbing enough to the nerves of the Chancelleries of all Europe.

Liszt, be-medalled and be-starred by nearly every crowned head, had his honourable obligations whether as a man of the world or as an artist, and he saw the risk of being compromised. But he had pledged himself to the little man downstairs, who with his hand-bag was keeping well in shadow as strangers passed out and in, starting in alarm at every knock. For Liszt the only thing was to put the best face upon it and smuggle Wagner into the Altenburg.

The Princess had sound reasons for not sheltering what seemed a lively explosive. Had she known it, he was merely a damp squib, politically, harmful enough for all that. Russian methods may not have been glaringly in evidence in Weimar, but she was conscious that they were there. She knew little of Wagner as a composer, but chiefly as a friend of Liszt's, so rivalry at this moment was not in her mind. But she was well alive to the danger of giving shelter to a refugee no matter his nationality. High treason was high treason in any latitude, and it was imperative that Wagner must be got rid of at all costs, whether a Saxon writ ran in Weimar or not.

In the short stay it was easy for Wagner, though difficult for his hosts, to pass from the unruffled and peaceful atmosphere of revolution to the devastating question of Richard himself and all his works. His hosts were uncomfortable, but the little man went on. The torrent was as if some one, let loose in an Encyclopaedia, insisted upon a discourse upon every article, from the letter A, with its inner meanings and ethical significance, down to Z, appropriately ending with the exclamation, "Zut!" It was not without effect, however, in distracting the Princess and turning her mind to *Tannhäuser* which she was anxious to hear again, and Wagner was not forgetful of her interest and sympathy.

It is a pity that we have not the Princess's comments on Wagner's excitable discourses—those entangled arguments and confused ideas of which later she could make little. That she was not unsympathetic at first is shown by the tone of the few letters to him that have been published. Throughout his life he seems to have been everlastingly addressing public meetings, sometimes with an audience of one, or none at all, and this tendency to break out antagonized many who would have preferred that he had burst into song instead.

The stay in the Altenburg of this fantastic begetter of theories was cut short by warnings from his wife that the police were out, and in connivance with friends of Liszt's, and some jugglery with a passport not his own, Wagner slipped off to Switzerland, and thence to Paris. Liszt had given him an introduction to Belloni, his secretary, but the letter begging for money was not long in arriving, and Liszt was hard put to it to satisfy Wagner's demands, with his wife's health as the plea.

In August, 1850, Liszt had given the first performance of *Lohengrin*, drawing down upon himself objurgations that should have been directed at Wagner. Meanwhile Hans von Bülow had come to Weimar, full of enthusiasm for Liszt, and wholeheartedly with Wagner—a brilliant lad with a great future, the best educated of the group. He had, besides, the candour of his years. Writing to his mother in 1850, he spoke of his attempt to explain to the Princess what Wagner meant by *Lohengrin*. When he referred to Wagner's outspoken ideas in his pamphlets she cried, " Ah, sir ! Don't talk to me of these great bêtises ? " In after days, whenever Wagner's name was mentioned, her favourite expression was " these great stupid things."

At this time she was all for Wagner's music, but scornful of his theories and prose writings. Fifteen months later, in a letter of January, 4, 1852, she showed herself circumspect about *Lohengrin*, possibly writing under Liszt's eye who may have detected early signs of that hostility which very soon was to be openly displayed. In this letter, however, she bubbled over with a description of a performance, giving an account of the physical endowments of the Ortrud, but stopping short of those ankles, " swoln and thick," which in some later and weightier prima donna must have caused a shudder to Hans Sachs and Walther in the shoe-fitting scene in the Third Act of *Die Meistersinger*.

It is no more than the plain truth that between the date of the " banker " letter and his stay in Munich in 1864, Wagner was showing himself at his very worst. Liszt may have been a little hasty in declaring his faith in him, but once pledged he could not go back, and though the two were to meet less than half-a-dozen times in these sixteen years, Liszt was performing Wagner's music whenever there was an opportunity. He was doing more, he was attempting to clear the air and soothe the feelings of those who had been wounded by Wagner's uncalled-for

Schwärmerei

asperities. Were it worth while to take a census of the epithets applied to Wagner the man, in the immense correspondence with or about him, the result would be overwhelmingly unfavourable. There is no question here of his music. It does not enter into this essay.

Liszt did not go to Paris in 1861 till after the *Tannhäuser* fiasco, probably having heard that Wagner had been setting everyone by the ears. It would appear, indeed, that Liszt was trying to avoid him, or at any rate to escape from any controversy that might affect his prestige. Then there was the Countess d'Agoult, with whom he lunched, and he had just been promoted from Officer to Commander of the Legion of Honour. In favour at the Court of the Tuileries, it would not have been wise to identify himself with Wagner, the political refugee, whose attitude towards the Parisian public was intolerant and intolerable. In spite of the patronage of Napoleon III, for whom Liszt always had the highest esteem, *Tannhäuser* had been a terrible failure, mainly owing to Wagner himself. It was his Sedan.

After this the correspondence was not regular: Wagner wanted money and Liszt was at his wit's end to know where to obtain it. He saw Wagner in Munich in 1864, living under the protection of Ludwig II, but to a correspondent about this time he said that he had had no direct news of him for more than two years and had not heard from him for three. This did not look like an immortal friendship. It must be pointed out, however, that in 1860 the Princess left Weimar for Rome, on divorce business, but Wagner must have been occupying her mind quite as much as he had been, when, ten years before, she spoke of his " bêtises."

CHAPTER IX

WEIMAR DAYS[1]

In a musical sense Liszt's ten years in Weimar were the most fruitful. Between 1849 and 1858 he had completed his twelve Symphonic Poems, his *Faust* and *Dante* Symphonies, the *Mass* for the Cathedral of Gran, and parts of larger and innumerable smaller works.

He had made Weimar a centre of all the arts, and every notable name in music, painting, sculpture and literature, was made welcome to the Altenburg.

There was friction with the Leipzig party, but tension nearer home, partly from his efforts to raise the standard of music, partly from his innovations in composition, partly too, from his persistent advocacy of Wagner. Besides, there was the anomalous position in which he had placed himself towards the Princess. It was a blow when the pair were cut dead ten years after all Weimar had been aware of their relationship. It is difficult to understand why this open ostracism had been postponed for so long. Liszt as the central figure in musical Germany, the Princess endowed with an intellect which attracted men of all shades of opinion, must have had many an enemy, begrudging their accomplishments, if not

---

[1] Occasional repetition is scarcely avoidable in a discussion of three characters whose orbits attract and repel.

their success. The suddenness of the untoward demonstration at the unveiling of the monument to Goethe and Schiller must have been premeditated. The year was 1857, and although it was not till 1860 that the Almanach de Gotha announced that Prince Nikolaus Sayn-Wittgenstein had divorced Carolyne in 1855, some one in Weimar with Russian connection, the Dowager Grand Duchess herself, most likely, must have been aware of this, and it is incredible that the Princess herself had not been informed of it officially.[1] For as we shall see, her mind was set upon obtaining the divorce when she went to Rome in 1860.

It was a year (1857) full of contrasted happenings. The outburst at Leipzig against *Mazeppa* has been mentioned. The newspapers were full of that Teutonic speciality—Hate. Then Liszt had to encounter the bitter hostility and disloyalty of Hiller and Joachim, and finally there was the insistence of the Princess that the *Dante* Symphony must be performed at a Dresden Concert, with disastrous results.

It was more encouraging that the year saw the marriage of his daughters: Cosima, to Hans von Bülow, and Blandine, the elder, to Émile Ollivier, a Parisian lawyer and afterwards Prime Minister, whose remark in 1870 about France going lightheartedly, "avec un coeur léger", to war with Prussia wrought his downfall.

[1] The matter will be dealt with more fully in Chapter XII.

Weimar Days

In the following year things were not improved by the conduct of Dingelstedt, the manager of the Weimar opera-house, who openly showed his ill-will towards a form of art with which officially he was immediately concerned. Hence the reception of Cornelius's *Barber of Bagdad*.

But there was a more serious matter in Liszt's preoccupations—this time connected with Wagner. The Wesendonck crisis had reached Liszt's ears, but there is not a hint in the correspondence between him and the Princess who were together when Wagner took his dismissal from Asyl. We may be sure that while Liszt may have been mute, the Princess could not have brought herself to hold her tongue on the subject of Wagner's shortcomings and anything that was derogatory. Although the few letters of hers to Wagner that have been preserved convey a sense of understanding and cordiality—probably inspired by Liszt—the good feeling was not sustained, and between her last recorded letter to Wagner and the Wesendonck affair there was a silence of three years. While she could write to him enthusiastically about *Lohengrin*, she changed her tune when she classed it with his "bêtises" as undramatic and inconsistent. Wagner's involved explanations of his theories became so intolerable to her that it was a blunder in tact to discuss them in her presence. Wagner was to her an unsolved riddle, a problem without a key.

Liszt's letter to him after he had left Zurich and Mathilde Wesendonck was a curt, dry note about his Austrian passport.

The Princess had seen enough of Wagner to be alive to the influence that threatened to demolish her plans. Liszt was her bondsman and she meant to keep him to herself. It might be bitter enough to find her schemes outrivalled by those of a man who was not allowing any scruples to stand in his way, but it was infinitely more serious that the man for whom she had sacrificed so much should be sacrificing himself for a cause which she detested since she could not comprehend it.

She knew all of Liszt's private life and the Wesendonck affair could not be concealed from her. It came as a hammer-stroke to the wedge that she was driving between the two men. But we are not allowed to know what Liszt wrote about the matter, if he wrote anything. Of this, at any rate, we may be certain that the Princess was confirmed in her estimate of Wagner's character.

It is singular that she did not see in the lives of others a reflection of her own. When, after the cut direct, Liszt threw all pretence and discretion to the winds and went to live under the same roof with her, she seemed to attenuate the position by considering Wagner's " flat blasphemy " as merely a " choleric word " in her own case.

CHAPTER X

THE VISITS TO WAGNER IN ZURICH

In the preceding Chapter a somewhat summary account has been given of the years that Liszt spent with the Princess in Weimar. We have now to turn back and review the brief occasions when Liszt and Wagner were together, and the almost unique moment in the lives of these three fantastics when they all met.

Liszt visited Wagner in Zurich for the first time in 1853. They had not met for four years. It was to be a real holiday for Liszt, away from the Princess—one to be counted perhaps among the *fugues*, but not *clandestine* in this case, for he reported minutely how the time was being passed.

He was met by Wagner and they nearly suffocated one another by embraces, Wagner sometimes " screaming like a young eagle, laughing, weeping, dancing for at least quarter of an hour ". Then Liszt continues : " He has very good rooms and has furnished them handsomely. There's a sofa or rather a *chaise longue* and small armchair in green velvet. He has the piano scores of *Rienzi*,

Tannhäuser, and *Lohengrin* superbly bound. He is inclined to luxury, but doesn't go too far—just as you [i.e. the Princess] didn't deprive yourself of your ornaments for the " Erholung " balls, etc. . . . He dresses rather smartly. His hat is white with a slight amount of pink in it, and there's nothing of the democratic style about him. He has assured me a score of times that he has completely broken off all relations with the réfugiés [after the Dresden and other contemporary Revolutions]. . . . His relations with musicians are those of a great General who has to drill a handful of tallow-chandlers. His logic in regard to artists is bitter and pitiless. As for me, he loves me heart and soul, and never stops saying, ' Look what you have made of me.' When it is a question of matters relating to his reputation and popularity he has leapt to my neck twenty times in the day ; then he rolls about on the floor petting his dog Peps, and talking nonsense to it all the time. He objurgates the Jews, a generic term in his mind, and in a wide sense. In a word, a great and magnificent nature—something like Vesuvius in eruption blazing up in sheaves of bouquets, pink and lilac. . . . To-day he wanted to kill the fatted calf and have a big feast. We had some trouble to keep down the cost and limit the invitations to ten or twelve." [It is to be remembered that at this time Wagner was forty years of age.]

The following day Liszt's comment was, " Wagner

PLATE II

RICHARD WAGNER

By permission of Messrs. Elliott & Fry, Ltd.

[*face p. 82*

The Visits to Wagner in Zurich

declares that he wants to keep open house from morning till eve while I am here. I am rather worried about the expenses that I am running him into, for there are always a dozen people at dinner at one o'clock and for supper at nine-thirty. . . . One of our common friends told me yesterday that when Wagner first came here he put everybody's back up by his behaviour, but when he found his feet he won his way into the esteem of the local people, and that after his rehearsals and concerts he became so amiable that no one could resist him. . . . Honours are in store for him and he has vowed to give up politics."

[But just twelve years later, in December, 1865, he was banished from Bavaria because he was suspected of having meddled in affairs of state, and in May, 1866, the clandestine visit of Ludwig II to him at Triebschen was ascribed rightly or wrongly to his interference in a delicate situation between Bavaria and Austria, which precipitated the Seven Weeks' War, culminating in the defeat of Bavaria at Sadowa.]

There is more in this report of Liszt's.

"His manner is decidedly masterful and his reserve is ill-disguised. Towards me the exception is complete and absolute. Yesterday he repeated, 'In my eyes all Germany is yourself,' and he never loses an opportunity of saying so to his friends. I fancy that you would take to his attractiveness.

He has frankly convinced himself that he is an extraordinary person whom the public only faintly and superficially appreciates. ... Among his followers and disciples is Karl Ritter, an absurd person, but for special reasons. The Ritter family make him an annual allowance [*Jahrgeld*] of 1000 écus, but at the rate at which Wagner is living I fancy he spends at least twice or thrice as much. Hermann [Liszt's valet] tells me that his wine-cellar is well filled, and Wagner has a pronounced taste for luxury and expensive habits."

From the foregoing it is clear that Liszt at this time had taken the measure of Wagner the man, and quite innocently and unconsciously was laying the foundations of that hostility on the part of the Princess towards Wagner that ultimately alienated all three from one another. Liszt with no assured income, unless he went back to the hated platform, was not reticent about Wagner's luxurious habits. Seven years later, that down-right Leipzig Cantor, Moritz Hauptmann, asked where on earth did Wagner get his money? He added that Liszt could not afford it.

It will never be known how much money Wagner ran through for mere personal caprices. Unrestrained in his extravagance in language, he was infinitely more extravagant in his attire and in his surroundings. For the joyousness of the world

The Visits to Wagner in Zurich   85

some letters of his to a Vienna milliner were published, in which he gave her instructions as to the colours and trimmings of his satin trousers and dressing-gowns, and there is a description of the style in which he decorated one of the rooms he was occupying in Munich. The taste was so grotesque that it would have "killed business" if initiated by the proprietor of a beauty-parlour or a manicure-boudoir. There was plenty of masquerade in the surroundings of King Ludwig II at Neuschwanstein, but even in his own dwelling Wagner had to keep up the show. It would be difficult to put a name to the character in which he saw himself. Cross-gartered Malvolio in his yellow stockings was fantastic enough, but he would have had to yield the palm to Wagner, pyjama'd like a chorus-girl in a revue bedroom-scene. What could Minna or anyone make of him?

In speaking of Wagner's pretty ways of throwing other people's money about, Liszt may not have been altogether surprised to hear of the Munich ménage, ten years later, to which the above paragraph refers.

With the kindest will in the world Liszt was now endeavouring to place his friend in the most favourable position, but the more astute Princess flooded the situation with her analytical search-light. She knew her Liszt: but this letter written in all loyalty and disinterestedness, told her more than it was meant to tell: just that "little more" that she wanted to be sure about.

In spite of the general air of festivity at the time of Liszt's birthday, October 22, his second visit to Wagner in Zurich in 1856 was not auspicious. The Princess was there and a distinguished company, with Frau Minna Wagner as hostess-in-chief.

Wagner was ill at ease. The Princess had gathered round her the brains of Zurich and their transcendental talk was over his head. He had to listen to better wits than his own, and with a bad grace had to surrender the seat on the rostrum that he regarded as peculiarly his. Sneer as he might at the gang of professors (Professorenwirtschaft) they at least could put him in his place and set him right upon many a subject about which he was prone to dogmatize. On abstruse questions he was but a second-rate competitor with the Princess: she knew it: he felt it. The background was not befitting for the man who, as years went on, refused to travel except in a carriage reserved for crowned heads: who was to gorge himself untidily at a table alone, while the ladies of the Court fed him obsequiously with sausage.

The Princess was at the height of her brilliancy here, with Liszt as much in the limelight as she, with dinners and parties and much piano-playing. On his birthday there was an improvised performance of *Die Walküre*, with supper, champagne, arguments:

Wagner and Liszt almost coming to blows over opinions about Goethe's *Egmont*.

In the midst of it all Wagner was of more than one mind, influenced by the person to whom he was writing. When the excitement had died down he wrote to Otto Wesendonck, "My companionship with the two ladies [the Princess and her daughter] and particularly with the Princess, has had a good effect upon me in the end. The example of the Princess's great kind-heartedness has attuned me to more gentleness and government of my so excitable temper, so that I am returning to my solitude as from a school, with the feeling that I have learned something."

There is an air of contrition about these reflections which makes us suspect that there had been an episode, perhaps more than one, in which Wagner had forgotten himself.

But in the same breath he complained to von Bülow of the serious interference between Liszt and himself, caused by the Princess's "awful Professor-hunting." "Seeing what the lady truly is, a monstrum per excessum of brain and heart, one cannot be cross with her long, only it needs Liszt's matchless temperament to stand such vivacity; with a poor devil like myself it often disagreed. I can't endure this everlasting racket." But Liszt has already told us the kind of "racket" that was more to Wagner's taste.

It is not at all unlikely that his scorn for the "Professorenwirtschaft" was due to some deeply read member of the craft having rent him before all the company for his intrusion into subjects in which he was frankly illiterate.

For all his recklesness in talk he was held in high esteem by Liszt, at this period at any rate. What we have been allowed to see of him has been an aspect of his nature that was scarcely pleasant. He has been made to appear, often by his own showing, as a man to be shunned, and yet there must have been something attractive about him that counterbalanced the defects of his character.

Although Liszt remained steadfast and did all in his power to further Wagner's interests, it was the Princess who began to drive the wedge between the two. It had been her ambition to see Liszt far above his fellows as a composer. She aimed too high, and her ideal, admirable as it was, was overshadowed by this other composer, without whom she had reckoned. Wagner repeatedly reproached Liszt for his weakness and for being easily swayed, but it did not occur to him that he himself was profiting by that weakness, and that had Liszt shown any strength of purpose Wagner would have been the first to feel it. But for that weakness he might not have become the man that in the end he did become. The fairy-tale of friendship between the two men has awkward chapters, years of silence over which no bridge of sentimentality can be cast. For all his professions of loyalty to Wagner, Liszt was a man of the world and he knew too well that the great issue that he had in mind was in jeopardy through the stupidity and ignorance of the man whose cause he had espoused.

With her high hopes thwarted, the Princess saw in Wagner the evil genius of her friend, and had a shrewd notion that he was gaining by the stimulus which Liszt in his person and in his work was unconsciously providing. So she had Liszt in her thrall partly by encouraging his compositions, partly by playing upon the streak of religiosity that seemed so strangely at variance with his mode of life.

CHAPTER XI

WAGNER AGGRIEVED

We have seen how Wagner conducted himself during Liszt's two visits to Weimar. This wonderful friendship was to oscillate between fatuous transports and petty grievances and unworthy complaints. At first there was something attractive about the man, unusual and exuberant. These qualities in him must have come as a welcome contrast in an environment which was ponderous in its way of thinking, without a glimmer of insight into the gaiety which could be extracted from the most solemn theme.

To many at first Wagner must have been like the opening of a window, to let in fresh air. But as time went on the atmosphere changed, and then it was wiser to keep the window shut. Just as the Princess's visitors had to "de-ventilate" themselves, as we shall see in Chapter XV, it would have been well if there had been a current to disinfect those airs of Wagner's which, loaded with biting fumes, poisoned those who had been most willing to help him.

Wagner's grievance was that Liszt did not seem to

take him too seriously, or at any rate to respond to his complaints. But now and then he did bring himself to realize that others had their troubles as well. (See his letter of May 2, 1854, in *Briefwechsel*, ii, 22.)

Five years later, February 23, 1859, he appears to have felt that in some respects he had gone too far. " I had heard, to my horror, how great your annoyance must be, and B.'s [von Bülow's] account confirmed my impression that you were deeply annoyed and grieved by ingratitude, faithlessness and even treachery. . . . I am aware that I have too little control over myself, and rely upon the patience of others to an undue extent. An occasional lesson, therefore, does me good."

Then he speaks of Liszt's having misunderstood him, and that he, Wagner, must have cut a very ugly figure. " That was proved to me by the effect I had upon you . . . and in my irritation I recognized my ugliness. These attacks of my violence ought surely to have calmed down by this time." Towards the end he begs Liszt to tell him more about himself and his worries. " Sink your pride for once and write to me as plainly and as comprehensively as I too frequently do to you, much to your annoyance." The letter runs to six-and-a-half pages of print : about 2200 words !

Liszt's reply, if there was one, is not at hand. Wagner wrote again, March 25, 1859, " I should no doubt have had news from you, if, in my last letter, I had not given you such a dose of gravy." (Ich . . . eine Suppe eingebrocht hätte.)

Liszt's retort, on April 6, 1859, may have been dictated by the Princess who was with him at the time at Weimar. The translation is Hueffer's. "Your dose of gravy, (dicke Suppe) as you put it, was not particularly palatable. At our next meeting I shall have to say much about it, unfortunately of the negative kind," (leider ablehnenes). A snap, unusual for Liszt, this.

In the same month Wagner scolds him for not sending him his new works, and does not like to read advertisements of *Dante* before he gets his copy. A note from Liszt giving the dedication of *Dante* to Wagner follows, which Wagner asks to be kept between themselves. Excepting Wagner's charge that Liszt had left him in the lurch, and a fine reply from Liszt, there is little to note till Wagner's letter to von Bülow of October 7, which shows the extent of the rift. The breach between Wagner and the Princess was complete.

The gist of the letter is as follows.

"It is hinted that since my acquaintance with Liszt's compositions I have become quite a different fellow in Harmony from what I was before. But when friend Pohl blurts out this secret to all the world at the head of a short analysis of the Prelude to *Tristan*, I cannot suppose that such an indiscretion was authorized. He might have shown us both more discretion, for I believe he compromised Liszt, though he gratified the Princess. I don't know in what style to write to Liszt. I worry myself for weeks, intending to write to him. All that I get from him is at most a reply, and about half the length of my letters. He doesn't bother about me. I talk about him as an excellent friend, but he does not talk about me. . . . ." He continues:

["You can enlighten yourself from his conduct as to what stands between Liszt and me. . . His *Dante* had been on sale for a month. I waited for the dedication copy and supposed that the delay was due to his exceeding me in extravagance when I sent him the dedication copy of *Lohengrin* in beautiful binding. Finally I got impatient and begged urgently for a copy. He sent me one. To my shame and confusion I saw that I was deceived as to the reason for the delay : the copy was as if it had come from the shop. Liszt had inscribed an extravagant, beautiful line to strengthen the dedication, but R. Pohl dared not allow it to be printed. There was not a friendly word [from Liszt] as an excuse. Now I learn that his *Mass* has been out for some time. He knows how keen I am about his work."][1] Wagner was now well on his way to become a Wagnerian.

The discrepancy about the dedication in the copy of the *Dante* is to be noted. To Liszt Wagner writes

[1] The passage between brackets is quoted in *Franz Liszt, ein Gedankenblatt*, von seiner Tochter, 2nd ed. Munich, 1911. It is singular that Frau Wagner should have shown up the pettiness of her husband towards her own father.

asking that the dedication shall be kept between themselves. To von Bülow he accuses Pohl of having suppressed it.

Von Bülow sent the letter to Liszt. What was his motive? Was it to let Liszt see what was in Wagner's mind, in the hope of bringing about a reconciliation? That, at any rate, would have done him honour, for, attached to both men and in constant correspondence with them, he felt that Liszt no more could be severed from Wagner than Wagner from Liszt, and he himself might be challenged to choose between them. On the other hand, there was the Princess in the background, and as he knew that nothing that Liszt said or did was kept from her, he felt that Wagner merited a sharp reproof, to be dictated by her, for his unreasonableness over trifles.

Perhaps Wagner was conscious that there was more than a suspicion that Liszt somehow had acounted for the glaring difference in style between *Lohengrin* and *Tristan*. His eagerness to study, but never to perform, Liszt's Symphonic Poems may have led his friends to ask if there was not something else underlying all this enthusiasm. There were numbers of musicians only too ready to discover flaws in the technique of either, and to trace them, if possible, to their source.[1]

---

[1] A fortnight later, on October 20, Wagner seems to have forgotten what he had written to von Bülow, for in his birthday letter to Liszt he said, "Your friendship to me is an indispensable necessity: I hold to it with every ounce of my strength."

Wagner Aggrieved

When Liszt received from von Bülow, Wagner's letter of October 7, he promptly communicated its contents to the Princess. It is evident that she had summed up Wagner fairly accurately and that she must often have discussed and disapproved of Liszt's having much to do with him.

Here is his letter to her of October 20, 1859.

"Hans has sent on Wagner's letter, the sense of which bears out your forecast. Without explaining himself exactly, and preserving a certain delicacy of language which he has not employed in other circumstances, he makes it clear that he wishes to part those whom God has joined together, namely you and me! He complains of my reserve, of the unbound copy of my *Dante* that I sent him six weeks after publication. That he has not received copies of my *Mass* and the Gipsy-book: [*Die Zigeuner und ihre Musik in Ungarn*] of some lines of Pohl on the subject of the Prelude to *Tristan* in which it is said that the harmonic tissue of the movement is influenced by a study of the Symphonic Poems, etc. etc. In fact he is trying to insinuate that you exert over me a regrettable influence and one contrary to my true nature. If Wagner has not the merit of inventing this stupid idea, I do not intend to share its absurdity. Every time he has tried to harp on this theme I have promptly shut him up—considering that he injures me trebly by so false an idea. He is now living at 16 rue Newton

Avenue des Champs Élysées. Perhaps you will see him. I almost urge you. But deal gently with him, for he is ill and incurable. That's why we must just love him and try to help him as much as we can."

But the Princess did not call. On November 23, Wagner wrote to Liszt from Paris that he had been deeply hurt (ungemein geschmerzt) because the Princess had not sought him out (aufzusehen). No further letter is given till Wagner's from Brussels at the end of March, 1860.

For all Liszt's single-mindedness towards his exacting friend the Princess, she was apprehensive lest he should become merely the cat's-paw of a man whose professions of devotion were not entirely disinterested. To her they were too transparent: to her Liszt was more than Wagner ever could be, echoing Wagner's oft-repeated phrase, "Liszt is more to me than I to him," a phrase which meant only one thing. Liszt could help Wagner in musical ideas, in purse and by performances of his works: Wagner never helped Liszt in anything.

While not musical in the sense that Liszt was musical, the Princess had the suspicion that Liszt's orchestral compositions were being closely studied by Wagner in order that he might learn not a little from them.[1] Not herself an expert, and unable to

---

[1] The extent of some of Wagner's borrowings is given in James Huneker's *Franz Liszt*, New York, 1911, pp. 141-144.

Wagner Aggrieved

lay finger upon direct evidence of influences, she nevertheless was on her guard. Wagner's professions of loyalty were tainted, and she wondered what was behind them. Wagner, too, was beginning to realize that he was meeting his match, and Liszt was striving to rid his mind of signs of an increasing tension.

Although he betrayed irritation, Wagner at times was in a state of fear, and he was afraid of two men, Liszt and Nietzsche.[1] Knowing undoubtedly in his mind that each was in some respects his master, he drained both in ideas. He encouraged Nietzsche's exuberance while appropriating his thoughts. The young Professor of Classical Philology was a gold mine of knowledge and learning, and Wagner was not the man to throw away the rare opportunity of extracting and minting every ounce—until found out. He suppressed Liszt on the platform as a composer, but upheld him in pamphlet and in letters which were too effusive to be sincere. He meant to have him and to hold him at all costs. It would be intolerable were Liszt to transfer his influence and patronage to any other, to Berlioz, for instance, and he tried to awaken in him a response to the tone of the letters which he addressed to him.

It is not without significance that the Princess referred to the correspondence between Goethe and Schiller as superficial. Clearly she had in her mind

[1] See *Richard Wagner as he Lived*, pp. 223, et seq.

the moment when the correspondence between Liszt and Wagner might assume an analogous character, and she resented the association of Liszt with a man who was laying waste the energy and substance of him with whom she had cast her lot.

For about a decade all was to go well at Weimar till the Russian divorce made its ugly appearance. But as far as can be ascertained Wagner had no hand in this. He was too busy with something more important—himself. He had the ear of the Press. With him the scribbling habit was not far removed from being a vice. He was oblivious of all consistency so long as he saw himself in print. When he was not cheap he was vulgar. His ill-timed and anonymous attack on *Judenthum* was just what was to be expected of so addled a brain.

On April 9, 1851, Liszt wrote to him thus; " Can you tell me, under the seal of the most absolute secrecy, whether the famous article on the Jews in music (*Das Judenthum in der Musik*) in Brendel's paper is by you?" Anonymous or not, Wagner's literary style was too pronounced to be concealed from one who knew him so well, and Liszt was not to be deceived.

Wagner's reply was anything but a well-reasoned justification. "You ask me about the *Judenthum*. You must know that the article is by me. Why do you ask? [I wrote] not from fear, but only to avoid that the Jews should drag this question into bare personality I appear in a pseudonymous capacity. I felt a long-repressed hatred for this Jewry, and this hatred is as necessary to my nature as gall is to the blood. An opportunity arose when their damnable scribbling annoyed me most, and so I broke forth at last. It seems to have made a tremendous impression and that pleases me, for I really wanted to frighten them in this manner. . . . Towards Meyerbeer my position is a peculiar one. I do not hate him but he disgusts me beyond measure."

And so on for a couple of pages of print. So the personal attack was to be only from Wagner's side. He was to be immune, of course. The article and the letter constituted a minute dissection of his mind and were valuable only to his enemies. Eighteen years later he was to " break forth " with even deeper violence by republishing the article with additions and this at a time when he was asking for contributions towards the building of the Bayreuth theatre, no matter from whom.

At this period (1851) in Liszt's letters to the Princess there is no reference to the onslaught, probably because Wagner was beginning to place himself in an unfavourable light, and Liszt did not wish to make matters worse. Liszt with his magical fingers had flung his musical ideas profligate abroad, and he was aware of the pilfering by, and the travesties of, the man who never ceased to acclaim him in public, but not in his musical scores, as his best friend.

CHAPTER XII

VOX ROMANA

Liszt was approaching his fiftieth year when two events of domestic importance occurred. In October, 1859, Marie, the Princess's daughter, made a brilliant marriage with Prince Konstantin Hohenlohe-Shillingsfürst, and a year later it came to light that Prince N. Sayn-Wittgenstein had divorced Carolyne. She was a free woman at last, with her daughter happily disposed of, and her ex-husband and his relatives no longer were in a position to slander her at the Russian Court. The procedure in the second case is not clear, for Liszt, writing to the Princess on November 23rd, 1860, quoted an advance copy of the Almanach de Gotha for 1861, just published, in which it was recorded that Prince Nikolaus, her husband, had divorced her in 1855, five years earlier.

This must have been something of a surprise. If Liszt had consulted the Almanach of 1855 and the following years he would have made the discovery that the divorce was not recorded in the Almanach till 1860. Further, in the copy for that year, and *for that year only*, he would have gathered the information that the Prince had contracted a second marriage in January, 1856, this time to Princess Marie, née Michailoff. In the copy for 1861, which Liszt saw, the divorce is mentioned, but not the second marriage, and no subsequent reference to the latter appears in the copies for the following years. Thus, as far as we are allowed to know, Liszt and the Princess were quite unaware of the divorce of 1855 and of the second marriage of 1856. It is hard to accept this. It is inconceivable that these facts were not known to some of their friends, for in every German household, especially in those linked with the nobility, there was no book so well-thumbed and dog-eared as the yearly Almanach de Gotha. With his association with Grand Dukes and titled folk of all ranks, Liszt must have noticed, dozens of times, the rigidity of Court etiquette and of the order of precedence, and as a host he must have consulted some Court chamberlain as to the seating of his guests at table. Seeing that the divorce was dated 1855, there must have been singular laxity on the part of the authorities to allow the Princess to push her claims for a divorce which had already been granted to her husband. At the same time there must have been indifference on the part of Liszt towards inquiries, an absence of curiosity on the part of the Princess, and a cynical prevarication on the part of those who encouraged her in her proceedings for divorce, well knowing that for these five years she had been a divorced woman. All three were inculpated, and it was left to the Vatican to play the last card.

The Princess, at all events, had the satisfaction of knowing that such ties as had existed, slender as they were, had been finally severed, so off she betook herself to Rome, for the business of making amends for the faux pas of thirteen years before. This broke up the establishment at Weimar, and Rome henceforth was to be her permanent headquarters. An odd woman this, intellectual, but capricious, worshipping two idols—never ideals—religion, which was to prove her eclipse, and Liszt, her ignis fatuus. Uncertain of him as a musician, and indifferent to the censoriousness of the Church upon themselves, she aspired to a marriage which, on the face of it, was ridiculous. She was no mate for Liszt: ultimately she was to him a species of Wagner in petticoats, smothered in incense and stale tobacco-smoke.

Her correspondence with Liszt then took on a colour that was nearly all black. If now and then she closed her eyes to his petits voyages, she exacted from him daily bulletins of his doings. Dreary reading they are, compiled as if according to schedule to please her who read them. In Weimar, when both were in residence there was no escape: he could not call his soul his own: he had to draw up, as it were, a specification of it, in an odour of sanctity that was tainted. But now, with the Princess in Rome, attempting to out-manoeuvre the most astute organization on the face of the globe in an effort to obtain sanction for her marriage, Liszt had to keep in tune. It might be said of him that the Vox Romana stop in that organ of his registered too incessantly to the keynote given out by the Princess.

Clearly she had him well in hand by this time. His letters in the latter part of the year, 1860, are a mixture of European politics with dealings with ecclesiastics. On the 6th of February, 1861, he wrote, " Mon examen de conscience m'a conduit à ressentir toute la monotonie de mes nombreuses fautes. Ma vie entière n'est qu'une longue Odyssée, si vous me passez cette comparaison, du sentiment de l'amour. Je n'étais propre qu'à aimer—et jusqu'ici hélas ! je n'ai su que mal aimer ! "

If he had had to review his past life to some one *sub sigillo*, that person must have been staggered by the procession of strange women unrolled from Liszt's memory—not by any means monotonous— from La Prunarède to Carolyne, with Marie d'Agoult the acknowledged mother of his children, Lola Montez, Kameliendamen, and many another unnamed who had entertained his caprices. He may have convinced himself of his sincerity when he wrote in the same month, " J'en remercie les Cardinaux, Messeigneurs et R. Pères de toute mon âme, et je me propose de mon mieux de devenir tout aussi ' Romano ' que vous ! "

" Basta, caro Liszt ! " is said to have been the exclamation of Pio Nono, after listening for five hours to his confession on his becoming an Abbé. " Go and tell the rest of your sins to the piano ! "

From this moment there was but one thought in the Princess's mind—marriage, and some position for Liszt for reorganizing the music of the Latin Church. She was not yet at work on that immense treatise, *Causes intérieures de la Faiblesse extérieure de l'Église*, which was to bring down on her head the thunders of the Inquisitors of the Index.

Liszt did not go to Paris for the performances of *Tannhäuser*—that fiasco which he compared with the reception of Cornelius's *Barber of Bagdad*, but on May 16 he admitted that the Princess had judged Wagner aright, and evidently unfavourably. Speaking of a letter which he had received from Wagner he wrote that whatsoever turn Wagner's affairs might take, he would hold himself aloof, adding, " Je vous dirai qu'Ollivier a écrit une lettre fort sévère à Mme. Wagner, qui, à ce qu'il parait, a fait des cancans[1] très déplaisants sur Blandine. Il

---

[1] Liszt's use of the word " cancans " was philologically correct. It had nothing to do with the *danses décolletées* in Paris in the Nineteenth Century, but was in vogue quite two hundred years earlier, applied to the slanderous and abusive language of shrews quarrelling with one another on their door-steps or out of the windows of projecting storeys in old Paris. As to its derivation the etymologists may well be left to their own " cancans."

est difficile que les relations se renouent après cela. Pour ma part, je ne m'en mêlerai point, l'expérience m'ayant trop enseigné l'inutilité des replâtrages ! "

Evidently Minna Wagner had been rather too free with her tongue. We are not told what it was all about.

Whatever the personal relations between Liszt and Wagner in Paris in May, 1861—and it is evident that Liszt was avoiding him—Liszt felt it his duty, in view of the opposition to Wagner at the time of, and subsequent to, the *Tannhäuser* fiasco, to make his profession of faith. This he did in a letter to the Princess of June 12, declaring his high admiration of Wagner's genius, which he had the honour to maintain in all circumstances during the last twelve years—recognizing in him the three qualities of theorist, poet and musician. " I have never written or said that I adhered to any contentious or upsetting (perturbatrice) theory, but at all times I have expressed my enthusiasm with which the Beautiful inspires me, and even everything that is beautiful. In the matter of art, theories have no importance to me . . . . Wagner is the dramatic poet and musician of Germany itself : that is enough for me to do him homage."

This, and the letter following, June 29, show that Liszt had recovered some independence of spirit, for in the second letter he enters into details of his meeting the mother of his children, but without a syllable of regret or recrimination, except her hint that he had prevented Cosima from following her true career, that of an artist !

The correspondence does not give a clue to the Princess's feelings on reading these letters. Liszt was too gentle in character to strike an attitude of defiance, yet there was a tinge of revolt in his declaration of loyalty to her arch-enemy, and in his long account of his meeting with one of her predecessors—that one with whom he had a more abiding link in Blandine and Cosima than with the Princess and all her bondieuseries. She perhaps was too deeply immersed in the black atmosphere, or interested in Liszt's association with Grand Dukes and petty nobility to notice the full significance of what he had to tell. At the same time there may have been more than a word of reproof, for there was ample time for a letter to have reached him in reply.

In spite of her preoccupations with Cardinals, she kept an eye on her belongings in the Altenburg, of the safety of which Liszt reassured her. But she must have asked him to be on his guard about "notre affaire," for on July 23 he wrote at length of the steps which he was taking to dissimulate.

"Have no anxiety about anything concerning my discretion. I haven't uttered a syllable to give rise to the suspicion that you are ' on rather good terms ' with [Cardinal] Antonelli, or that he has written to me or that I am reckoning on so-and-so's protection. You know it has always been my way never to show what would be agreeable or advantageous to myself. Consequently for the best of reasons I don't talk too much. When I am asked for news of you I reply somewhat dryly that your health is good and that the climate of Italy suits you. There's no risk in saying this and it doesn't encourage people to ask more. If by chance that happens, I pay the indiscreet and importunate people back in their own coin .... It has often reached my ears that the marriage should take place in Italy. I have always replied evasively, without ever mentioning a place, giving rather the idea that a marriage which has been so often postponed may be so again, and perhaps indefinitely. I don't see the need for this or that person to be told about what interests us. There's plenty of other things to talk about besides that .... Nobody will know anything about your concerns, your plans, your undertakings, your friends, etc. Your letters are always under lock and key."

Tongues evidently were busy, and the presence of Liszt in a small place like Weimar, without his unspeakable and conspicuous companion, set gossip agog, snatching at any windlestraw to discredit the woman who, despite the slackness of her morals, had queened it with imperious rein over everybody.

The conclusion of the whole matter of the marriage was more a coup de théâtre than a coup de tonnerre.

Both had occupied the stage to such an extent that a thunderbolt, a flash of lightning, was merely as a spray of limelight upon their tortuous lives.

On Liszt's fiftieth birthday the ceremony was to take place in the fashionable church, San Carlo al Corso, which was decorated for the occasion. But on the eve of October 22, 1861, a messenger from the Vatican asked for the dossier of the Princess and of Liszt, and thereon Canon Law stiffened, obdurate and inexpugnable. Late that evening Liszt was reminded of his life-long shortcomings : the Princess, for all her associations with Cardinals and Prelates, was told that re-marriage after divorce could not be tolerated, and the altars of San Carlo were despoiled of their festive garb. In the night the blossoming symbols, to which the Princess in her white hair had given so much thought, were removed, and Society was robbed of what would have been an interesting and curious function.

So the Princess shut herself up with her theological treatises in her unventilated, sunless flat in Rome, while Liszt sought the no less insanitary air, as it then was, of the Roman Campagna and the Villa d'Este, to write a fantasia on some forgotten opera.

CHAPTER XIII

RÖMISCHE BRILLE

If the Princess had set her heart upon the marriage, to Liszt as we know him it was, as it were, merely a façon de parler, like his other adventures. Although both had seen things through what he called "Römische Brille," her Roman spectacles had been the more roseate. All her efforts, her interviews with highly-placed ecclesiastics, all the arguments and precedents, came to grief in the blackness of a Roman night. Her rooms had been buzzing with Cardinals and attendant Monsignori, as if some Consistory were assembled there, and all Rome was a-tiptoe for the smart wedding, curious to see how the much-talked-of bride of forty-two would carry herself, and how many orders and decorations the great pianist would wear. No young bride was more expectant than she when late at night there came the crushing interdict. To all appearance she had felt certain of her ground.

With her ransackings of Canon Law, with authorities at her elbow either to encourage her along a path which they well knew led nowhere, or to gain a zealous propagandist, she ought to have discovered, and others must have been aware, that she was heading for a trap. The thing was glaringly insuperable. Ecclesiastical law could not be shaken into countenancing the re-marriage of a divorced person, but while the Cardinalate with eyes shut might make an exception in the case of a lady who was an ardent proselytizer, the Holy See was inflexible and down came the white, oft-kissed slipper of Pio Nono.

So the hangings and decorations of San Carlo had to be swept away, and Roman Society was left with the grievance that the toilettes specially ordered for the occasion might be out of fashion for the next ceremonial function.

Liszt, with all his love for female finery, could not have realized the effect of this when so important a part of the social programme fell through. To do him justice he had begged for a quiet ceremony with only a friend or two present, but the Princess was bent on a public display with all the paraphernalia of the rite.

After the veto she remained in Rome: Liszt also for the most part, till August, 1864, when he went to a musical festival at Carlsruhe. Little can be gathered from his published correspondence with the Princess at this time. Although they were not living under one roof they were meeting constantly, often daily, and his notes to her dealt mainly with appointments, commissions, meals, and the like.

There is one letter, however, written from the Villa d'Este (July 1864) which shows Liszt in a mood that was unusual for him. It conveys the impression that the Princess had been reproaching him for want of candour concerning the people he was meeting, and for withholding from her his preoccupations.

"How can I convince you," he wrote, "that I have no need of anything or anybody except yourself and myself? I have said it, repeated it, demonstrated it and proved it a hundred times in all simplicity and truth. Why, then, wound me in not believing in my complete good faith?"

To this no solution is forthcoming, but it may be inferred that the Princess was exacting on all points and was determined that nothing in his life was to escape her. Whatever it was that called for Liszt's remonstrance, it reveals irritation on his part, and the date is significant, for in March her husband, Prince Nikolaus Sayn-Wittgenstein died, and she was absolved from all bonds imposed by the Church. She was now free to marry if she had a mind to, but Liszt did not refer to the matter. She had other plans.

Back in Germany again, after an absence of three years, Liszt wrote at length of his movements and his doings, with Cosima von Bülow and another as his companion. With Wagner he had not had direct communication for two years, and in August,

1864, he was meeting him again after a separation of three.

Wagner by this time had found a patron in King Ludwig II of Bavaria, and was making the most of his opportunities. He had won Liszt's interest by showing him some letters that the King had written to him. Liszt was impressed by their tone, without the more sober reflection that they were scarcely what a crowned head not out of his teens would be expected to write to a composer—to any man, indeed—past his fiftieth year. Still he clung to his subject. Wagner was to Liszt " le Glorieux." " Nothing between us is changed. The exalted fortune which at last he has encountered will mollify as much as possible some asperities in his character . . . He has become a Bavarian subject. . . . His *Meistersinger* is a masterpiece of humour, wit and lively grace. It is happy and beautiful, like Shakespeare."

Praise of this kind was not the ideal sedative for a resentful woman. She had not forgotten the Zurich visit, and if music in Liszt was to be surrendered to this protégé of a mad and youthful king, and no longer to be the mainspring of her ambition, there were Octaves, not musical, which she could play off on him in another direction. Unstable as had been her propaganda for Liszt the composer, the centre of gravity was shifting round to herself, and she kept fostering the idea. With marriage fading into the grey distance and with close association with the clerical party, the assiduous Princess played upon him with her blunt fingers and led him to a point when, Wagner or no Wagner, she would see him not in the dull robe of an abbé, but in the blinding splendour of a Cardinal . . . if it could be managed.

Liszt returned to Rome at the end of October, and the next six months were given up to devotion and his preparation for receiving the tonsure and admission into the four Minor Orders as Doorkeeper, Reader, Exorcist and Acolyte. Candidates for the first had to be learned in the rudiments of the faith and to be able to read and write (*saltem grammatice*) : for initiation into the other Orders an understanding of Latin was required.

Three days before the ceremony, in a note to the Princess, he mentioned that the Pope had spoken to him of the necessity of studying Latin, and in the same note he told her that he had tried on his new soutane in the presence of Monsignore Hohenlohe with complete success. Was this the garment to which his tailor had stitched the loops and beckets (as a photograph shows) for the exhibition of his many orders and decorations ?

Liszt no doubt was sincere in his wish to be attached to the church, even though the bonds were slender and fragile enough to be snapped. But it is strange to think that on the eve of the religious ceremony he should have sat at the piano in the Palazzo Barberini to play before a brilliant company his arrangement of Weber's *Introduction to the Dance*, and Schubert's *Erlking*.

Scarcely had there been time for him to realize the significance of the step which he had taken than a letter arrived from his mother in Paris, dated May 4, 1865. It was an acknowledgement of his of April 27, in which he told her that he had received the four Minor Orders two days before.

There was something pathetic, something very touching, in the way she addressed him as her " dear child." She had heard rumours of his decision and was deeply hurt when people talked to her about it. Perhaps with her knowledge of his past affairs and those children of his whom she had been looking after, she may have feared that he had gone so far as to cut himself off from them all, and when he himself confirmed the news she burst into tears. In her mind this bent of Liszt's was no new thing: she could recall symptons of it when he was a lad, but fortunately he had been dissuaded from a vocation for which her motherly instinct told her he was unfitted. She may not have grasped the nice distinction between the Minor Orders and the priesthood, associating his action with vows that were irrevocable. As things were he had merely crossed the threshold, and there was no pledge to hinder him if he chose to turn back.

Of Liszt's mother we know little. His references to her are scanty. Born in 1791, Anna Lager was only twenty when she gave birth to her world-famed son, and she was approaching her seventy-fifth year—Liszt's age at his death—when she wrote that gentle letter to him. It shows how she loved her " dear child," and how proud she was of his career.

She died on the 6th of February, 1866. Liszt presumably was in Rome, constantly seeing the Princess, and this may account for the absence of references to the event. What he said then was all that there was to be said, for when he had to go to Paris, he wrote to the Princess of March 6, a letter which is a mixture of politics, newspaper business, dinners, saints' days, masses, déjeuners, prices of tickets and box office receipts, with a casual allusion to some of the people who were at his mother's funeral, ending with a request for the *Osservatore* if it should contain an article about his *Dante* Symphony. This confusion of thought was characteristic when scribbling (the word was his own) his daily " bulletin " to the Princess. It was only when there was a matter for argument that he adhered to a sequence of ideas, and these were seldom in consonance with hers.

Early in February, 1864 he expressed gratitude to his son-in-law, Émile Ollivier, in whose house

Frau Liszt had been living, and about the same time to Émile's brother, Adolphe, for the care they both had taken of his mother. From these and from two other contemporary letters it would appear that he had been warned of his mother's illness too late. At the same time, to remove any suspicion of indifference on Liszt's part, it must be remembered that the journey from Rome to Paris included a passage by sea to Marseilles. In his letters there are constant references to the length of time spent in wearisome journeys.

CHAPTER XIV

ENTER COSIMA

To understand the situation that arose between Hans von Bülow, Cosima Liszt and Richard Wagner, it is necessary briefly to give a preliminary outline. Hans was destined for the law, but through the encouragement of Liszt and Wagner entered upon a musical career. While they were in Berlin Blandine and Cosima were his pupils in music. In August, 1857 he married Cosima, then in her twentieth year. His age was twenty-seven. There were three children, Daniela, afterwards married to Professor Thode, Blandine II, afterwards Countess Gravina, and Isolde, born in 1865, who married Kapellmeister Beidler. Exactly fifty years after her birth a case was fought in the German courts, when it was decided that although she had been always recognised as Wagner's daughter, she was legally von Bülow's. She died in 1919 of consumption.

At this point the year that is of interest is 1864, when Wagner was the guest in Munich of Ludwig II. At the close of the preceding year he was in Berlin with the von Bülows. While Hans was rehearsing for a concert, Wagner and Cosima went for a drive together, and thereafter all barriers were down. With his influence over the insane king, it was a simple matter for Wagner to secure a Court appointment for von Bülow, so that he, and Cosima, of course, would be permanently resident in Munich. This provided the opportunity. Von Bülow's health was in a critical state. No definite reason was given; but knowing now a little more of the situation that had arisen, we might not be wide of the mark in assuming that his nerves were being worn to shreds by Wagner. Wagner, for all his self-commiseration, had no nerves whatsoever when a woman was in the case. Cosima, too, was losing patience with her husband, and took it upon herself to order Wagner's life, opening his letters, superintending his correspondence, and keeping at a distance importunate visitors.

Successful with Liszt's daughter, Wagner attempted success in another direction. He encouraged Ludwig in his monstrous follies and extravagances. The Court and then the people of Munich, suspicious of a revolutionary who dared not put foot in Saxony for fear of arrest, began to see in Wagner a meddlesome adventurer who was helping the king to drain the Treasury dry, and might at any moment influence him; with disaster to the State. The newspapers began to speak out.

Enter Cosima 119

Wagner, with Cosima not far off, attempted to reply to the charge that he was playing with Ludwig as Lola Montez had played with Ludwig's grandfather, and the order went forth by proclamation that Wagner must be banished from Bavaria. So he had to make another of his ignominious exits. By the middle of 1866 he was installed at Triebschen with Cosima and the three von Bülow children, the youngest being the Isolde already mentioned.

It is inconceivable that Liszt could have been wholly ignorant of a situation that affected the honour of his daughter and of the son-in-law to whom he was greatly attached. In touch with musicians he must have turned aside at every hint of scandal. His part in the crisis was not specially courageous. He was enough a man of the world to know that for all his " glorification " of Wagner, a king's favourite is not banished at a moment's notice without grave cause. Besides, his newly acquired ecclesiastic status did not cancel old scores. He had met the Countess d'Agoult in April, 1866, and she had threatened to publish her Confessions,[1] which he said would consist of "poses et mensonges ". There must have been some heat in their interviews, for in writing to the Princess he said that he had to put the question downright between Truth and Falsehood, and that to

---

[1] She published her *Souvenirs, 1806-1833*, in 1877.

have further intercourse with a mind like hers would be an act of immorality. Clearly he had not recovered from his resentment at being depicted as Guermann in her novel *Nélida*. This was an ancient wound and it rankled. Writing from Weimar on June 18, 1870, he spoke of Disraeli's *Lothair*, then just published, and expressed himself strongly about personages in real life being introduced under thin disguise into works of fiction as Disraeli had done.[1] He said that for thirty years he had protested against Balzac's *Béatrix* and Daniel Stern's *Nélida*.

As for his meeting with the Countess in 1866 he admitted to having spoken to her with some violence " Unfortunately there's no means of saying certain things nicely to people whom they wound. It isn't with strokes of a fan that one performs surgical operations."

It was one thing, however, to speak plainly to the Countess, but quite another to handle her daughter—and his. It was twenty-two years since he had separated from the mother, and the publication of events that occurred about the time

[1] *Lothair* was published in May, 1870. Liszt's letter is dated from the following month. It is unlikely that his knowledge of English was wide enough for him to have read it, and it is probable that he knew of its contents only by hearsay. Behind his objection to the introduction in a novel of well-known people under fictitious names lay something deeper—his resentment of the way in which Disraeli had handled certain spiritual forces in England of his time. See the important chapter in Buckle's *Life of Disraeli*, vol. v. p. 151, London, 1920, in which the novel is analysed.

Enter Cosima

of the separation—that Lola Montez affair cropping up again—not only would have compromised him and led to his total eclipse, but also would have put him in a false position in regard to the Church. It would have been worse than false : it would have been grotesque. He was too faint-hearted to throw down the gauntlet to the Countess, in spite of his brave words.

He had forgotten that of the four Minor Orders one was that of exorcist, whose business it was to rid those possessed of devils—energumeni, so called—but while he might be able to deal with one, he would need to consult the authorities how to manage three. The dilemma had one horn too many. A failure in every respect outside music, a poor lover, an indifferent parent who left his children to the care of others, Liszt wrapped himself in his pseudo-priestly garments and betook himself to the stuffy apartments of the Princess, there to be drugged and anaesthetized in a thoroughly septic atmosphere. She might read him to sleep with chapters of her pretentious and inexhaustible opinions upon church matters ; she might never have heard of the "triangle of error," Liszt's *pons asinorum*, but in the background, little as he dreamt of it, there was a young brain, not yet in her thirtieth year, who had seen him through and through. That was his daughter Cosima. She had meant to go her own way ; she had finished with him who had begotten her without a name by a lady to whom he was not married. Small wonder, then, that she was making the most of her life. And before that terror of a daughter Liszt flinched.

Shriven as he felt himself to be, daily if not hourly, in his reports to the Princess, that self-appointed keeper of his conscience, it was easy to cast his burden upon anyone whomsoever in scriptural terms, but the bearer of the burden, such are the ways and customs of evil, might find himself in the law courts, an unwilling victim.

But things had gone too far. A child had arrived. At last Liszt discovered a motive for acting, so in October, 1867, he made up his mind, and with the moral support of Richard Pohl set out for Triebschen. What took place during the interview with Wagner has never been made known. All that Liszt would admit afterwards was that " it was as if he had seen Napoleon at St. Helena."

So that glorious friendship between the two men, spoken of as the most perfect that an uninstructed world had ever seen, was broken, not to be resumed till after the laying of the foundation stone of the Bayreuth Theatre in 1872, and even then never as the world would like to imagine it.

Von Bülow's attitude was incomprehensible. He was actually a guest of Wagner at Triebschen after Cosima had left him. He was actually in the house when Wagner's first child by Cosima was born. "My dear wife was happily delivered of a healthy little girl (Nr. 4!)"—that is, he represented that the infant was his own fourth daughter. Through out the spring and early summer of this critical year, 1867, he was constantly referring to "my wife," apparently making an effort to shield her by keeping up a show of happy relations. He had conducted the first performance of *Tristan* in 1865, *Tannhäuser* and *Lohengrin* had been performed under him in 1867, and he conducted the first performance of *Die Meistersinger* in 1868. Wagner accepted these after he had stolen von Bülow's wife.

It is easy to construct theories: to say that the bond between von Bülow and the betrayer was music. That will not suffice. The bond did not exist between Liszt and Wagner, for some of the hardest things said about Wagner came from Liszt. There was something which cannot be fathomed. If ever letters are forthcoming for future generations, in them, perhaps, there will be found the reason for von Bülow's complacent disinterestedness.

To complete the chronicle at this stage it need only be said that in June, 1869, Siegfried Wagner was born, that in July, 1870, von Bülow divorced his wife, and that five weeks later she was married to Wagner, an event which Liszt learned only from the newspapers. She had not the grace to let him know. Further, as she knew that in her church—

the Roman—the re-marriage of divorced persons was forbidden, she slipped the noose from her neck and turned Protestant for the occasion. This perhaps, struck deeper in Liszt's heart than any of those trivial questions of adultery with which he was only too well acquainted.

CHAPTER XV

LA PRINCESSE CHEZ ELLE

The veto on her marriage to Liszt had driven the Princess further into the arms of the clerical party. She did not avail herself of the canonical freedom consequent upon the death of her husband in Russia. Liszt, as we have seen, was granted the four Minor Orders. This step, though it did not carry with it the privileges and obligations of the priesthood, was sufficient for him. It gave him a certain cachet in the eyes of some who regarded it as a triumph to have swept into the fold a musician with a world-wide reputation. Others, like his son-in-law, von Bülow, discerned beneath the soutane the Liszt of old, unchanged and unchangeable. It was after a concert in the Cathedral of Jena that Borodin wrote dryly to his wife, "On voit que l'Abbé n'avait guère rompu avec ses habitudes profanes," an observation due to Liszt's practice of paying marked attention to some one pupil—on this occasion a certain Vera—to the indignation and fury of the rest.

From the date of his admission to the Orders—it can hardly be called submission—on April 25, 1865 till his death, Liszt wrote over 700 letters to the Princess. Although for the most part they were full of expressions of affection and references to two hearts beating as one, there often was overmuch talk of Royal Highnesses, Grand Dukes and Saints, in this strict order of precedence, combined with time-tables, itineraries, and church-visitings.

To understand the person to whom they were addressed we must take a glimpse at the Princess in her Roman surroundings. What her letters to him were, we can gather only from his stray allusions to criticisms which do not seem always to have erred on the side of mildness. That any of them, from fifteen to twenty pages in that flourishing scrawl of hers, took him a whole morning to digest was not the complaint of Liszt alone. There were other victims. She was scribbling interminably—scribbling. Adelheid von Schorn—we shall see how she came to know—said that she kept two compositors fully employed and gave a list of forty-five of her works, all ecclesiastical. To be done with them at once a few may be mentioned.

Entretiens pratiques à l'Usage des Femmes du Monde, in one volume: more *Entretiens pratiques à l'Usage des Femmes du Grand Monde pour la durée d'une Retraite spirituelle,* this time for ladies of the "grand Monde," in eight volumes: *Simplicité des*

PLATE III

PRINCESS CAROLYNE SAYN-WITTGENSTEIN IN ROME

[face p. 126

La Princesse chez Elle

Colombes, Prudence des Serpents : *quelques Réflexions suggérées par les Femmes et les Temps actuels*. Her masterpiece in twenty-four volumes, no less, was *Causes intérieures de la Faiblesse extérieure de l'Église*, or in German, *Ueber die inner Gründe der äussern Schwäche der Kirche*. We shall hear a little about this work now and then. A few copies were printed for friends and learned men, but the public issue was not to appear till twenty-five years after her death.[1]

A fair output for a woman, for anybody, in 22 years. If that dread engine, the dictaphone, had been in use, it is reasonable to imagine its being " returned to the works " every week or so, for rest and repair.

As for herself, there are accounts from various sources which enable us to reconstruct the scene. She had taken over a flat in Rome from its former occupant with furniture and fittings as they stood. Each visitor without exception, even Liszt himself, had to stand for ten minutes by the clock in an outer room to be de-ventilated (sich auslüften) and rid himself of the dubiously fresh air before he could

[1] And to think that of all these not a copy is catalogued in the British Museum ! The good lady's name appears only once in *Aus der Glanzzeit der Weimarer Altenburg* : *Bilder und Briefe aus dem Leben der Fürstin Carolyne Sayn-Wittgenstein*, herausgegeben von la Mara. Leipzig, 1906. This book refers only to the Weimar period. For the Roman days we have the descriptions of Rohlfs, quoted by Kapp (p. 503) and Malwida von Meysenbug's *Der Lebensabend einer Idealistin* (first edition 1898). See p. 144 for reference to this lady.

be admitted to the Presence. That anyone survived after a mephitic whiff of the Princess's salon must be put down to an ever watchful Providence. Into this Paradise of Tainted Devices Liszt stepped, day after day, and night after night.

After the unpurification the visitor entered a room from which all daylight had been excluded. There, like a spider squatting in its web, sat Carolyne Sayn-Wittgenstein, writing by lamplight, dressed in all the colours of the rainbow, with streamers of ribbons from what a visitor—herself a woman—called her " hateful cap." Books ruled the walls, the chairs, the floor.[1] Her fingers held a cigar specially made double the length for her use. There were flowers in abundance, and a large bowl of sweets and chocolate from which she helped herself, munching when she was not smoking. There was a grand piano, too, so placed that it was difficult to pass between it and the wall. On a table were set innumerable busts of Liszt, and beside her there were relics and a whole shop-windowful of bondieuseries, the *pretantaine usuelle de sacristie*, that might have been picked up in the Via Propaganda Fide, hard by.

The taste of the former occupant was proved by the pictures of ballet-girls left enframed on the walls. If in the dead hours these damsels should have come to life and flitted about the room, there would have been many a giggle as they peeped into the Prin-

[1] This imitation of Sir Walter's famous line may be completed appropriately with " For men below and saints galore."

La Princesse chez Elle

cess's vellum-bound copies of such world-renowned authorities on moral theology as Sanchez and Liguorio. Liszt, little expert in Latin, would have had no curiosity: these theologians had nothing to teach him. In their arguments he was above all Latin. He knew as much as they. There was nothing in the *Compendium* to startle him.

Yet while he was in Rome he could not detach himself from the woman who had moved all Heaven, not to mention that Higher Power, the Vatican, to permit the marriage. When, however, the opportunity arrived, she had become so steeped in casuistry that she was able to argue herself out of all thoughts of matrimony. She was resolved to profit by the lesson: whether her voluminous writings were to find grace in the eyes of the Censors of ecclesiastical productions will be seen later.

It is difficult to discover what the Princess's exact position in Rome was. She was rarely out of doors except for occasional drives, and she seems to have looked to Liszt, as her alter ego, to fulfil the obligations which she was too much occupied to observe. She had always an alibi ready, with Liszt in the part of proxy when high matters were afoot.

At first there was no thought of her permanent stay in Rome, but gradually she yielded to the fascination of the Eternal City, and it was more comfortable to find herself courted in Rome than

K

"cut" in a dull little place like Weimar. Liszt had rooms hard by in the quarter of the Via del Babuino, with his meals sent in, but the enervating atmosphere and the demands of the Princess were making heavy drafts on his freedom. She complained that he was indolent and frittering away his existence, but she did not ask herself if it was not she who was to blame. She tried to get him appointed Director of the Papal Music, but this proposal was wrecked by the opposition and ignorance of the Roman Cardinals, and the Pope, Pio Nono, had no mind to thwart them. Liszt was on good terms with him, but after his death he had no further relations with the Vatican Some Prelates were not afraid of plain speaking. Monsignore Strossmayer, who had long held out against, though he ultimately accepted, the doctrine of Infallibility, said of Pius IX that he was too ignorant to discuss serious affairs. With his successor Leo XIII, Liszt had no dealings.

It was Monsignore, afterwards Cardinal, Hohenlohe, who saw that Liszt's character was bound to deteriorate with close association with the Princess. In after years Liszt used to complain that she could not be induced to abandon her slovenly ways, and move into apartments more befitting her rank. To provide for Liszt's comfort the Monsignore invited him to the Villa d'Este at Tivoli, where he had put in order a suite of rooms for him. It was here, with its wonderful views, that Liszt was to live when in Rome. About seventeen miles from the City, with only the cheap and uncomfortable service of the public *vetture* twice daily, he had an excuse for not coming into Rome too often, for the expensive carriages were far beyond his pocket.

Although his notes and letters to the Princess, almost at all times, were full of soulful exhortations, now and then they were but skin—or rather soutane—deep. It was well enough for him to write in 1861, that in five days he would find in her " patrie, foyer et autel," and no doubt for the first years they were on good terms, except when there arose two unfortunate topics, Wagner and the Church.

CHAPTER XVI

CAUSES INTÉRIEURES—BONDAGE

In an earlier Chapter (XI) a letter from Wagner to von Bülow was quoted, which the latter sent on to Liszt. It stares one in the face that Wagner's most ardent desire was to keep in touch with Liszt and Liszt's creative powers, while striving to remove the impression, obvious to all musicians, that the style of *Tristan* was not the logical or artistic outcome of the style of *Lohengrin*, its immediate predecessor.

If the progress of any art is examined, there is no example of a volte face from one style to another without some explanation, without the penetration of some influence. The passing of a woman, a Mathilde Wesendonck, or even a housemaid, through a man's mind, across his efforts, cannot inaugurate a new system of harmony in music or displace the old. Music, no matter by whom, leads to music in another, and what Wagner heard through the mind of Beethoven, Weber, Spontini, Meyerbeer, and dozens of others, became sublimated in his own.

With Liszt it was a different matter. No theorist, he trusted to his ear, and his ear was unusual, while Wagner, the greater in invention and technique, thirsted for the support of him who was the richer in thought.

If it was clear to the Princess that there was a striking gap between *Lohengrin* and *Tristan*, it must have been twenty times more obvious to trained musicians, and though later there were indications of direct borrowings, at this time there was sufficient material in Liszt's Symphonic Poems to cause Wagner to study them closely. They were almost the only contemporary music that interested him. And they, be it noted, had been written before *Tristan*. It had been observed as a tragic fact that for all that Liszt did for Wagner, Wagner never performed a Symphonic Poem of Liszt's, and that in the concerts for the Bayreuth funds, Wagner never conducted a Liszt work. This boycotting of his friend's compositions is inexplicable, unless it was that he feared that the more analytical in his audiences might detect, or imagine that they detected, Liszt's influence. Apart from all questions of policy, Wagner had nothing to be alarmed about, and Liszt recognized this, though there had been enough and more than enough to embitter him against the man himself. Against his music he would not tolerate a word.

The resumption of relations between the two men

was viewed by the Princess with misgivings. The warmth of the letters exchanged in 1872—letters which she demanded to see—the invitation to Bayreuth and Liszt's generous reply, seemed to light up a flame which she hoped had been quenched when Liszt left Triebschen and an unrepentant daughter. So, after all, something *had* been in Liszt's mind during these years of silence. The flame had been slumbering, and though it was never to give out its old warmth, it was a danger signal. The Princess felt that something was slipping from her.

Two influences were at work : double antagonisms. Liszt was leaning towards Bayreuth and Wagner, and she hated both. She herself, with her slipshod bombastic style, was dabbling in theological questions to which Liszt, quite doubtful of them, was opposed. He was holding to the discipline and letter of the law, deprecating her assumption of authority on matters well left to those whose business it was to investigate them.

Although later on the Princess vetoed any discussion of her writings, she evidently was in the habit at one time of going through them with him. One book, indeed, *La Matière dans la Dogmatique Chrétienne*, was dedicated to him, "À Monsieur l'Abbé Liszt, Grand-Croix de hautes Ordres, etc." It was dated 1871. In acknowledging it he said that on this occasion he would read it from cover to cover. He remarked the list of her publications

Causes Intérieures—Bondage

on the last page, twenty volumes of which were essays on various subjects. "To think of this productiveness in the midst of your thousands of other duties!"

Then in February, 1872, in regard to a pamphlet of 117 pages, *L'Exposé de la Musique d'Église* (sic), he mildly suggested her postponing its publication till the autumn, as he humbly proposed to go through it with her, "to make it as perfect as possible." It was quite as much his affair as hers. The subject seems to have been dropped, but the Princess had been criticizing something that she had heard about him, for he wrote, "I shall try to follow your wise advice not to let the man be out of harmony with the artist, and to affirm my faith by my conduct and works. Just forgive me if I don't share certain illusions about my public position. I am tied up between Pest and Weimar. I have nothing to look for elsewhere."

In July, 1872, he wrote from Weimar, "Many passages in your last two letters need thinking over. I will try to profit by them in spite of the difference in our points of view." Frequently he was to repeat these expressions as the years went on. From the date of this letter, following his sending her copies of his and Wagner's letter about the laying of the foundation stone of the Bayreuth theatre, we may assume that the Princess's "last two letters" were not unconnected with this event.

Liszt was wholly within his province in an rapprochement with Wagner: the Princess had no province: not even the rank of Chanoinesse, which might have led her censors to view her efforts with an eye compassionate in talk, but severely critical of cold print. Both she and Liszt had the Church at heart. He was strictly orthodox, outwardly at any rate, and was soon to be raised to the rank of titular Canon by his friend Hohenlohe, Bishop of Albano, a rank which entitled him to wear the purple, a distinction never assumed in public, for he was "porporato" only when photographed.

She, immersed in the Patrologia, blundered headlong into matters historical, canonical, theological, till, as will be seen presently, she received the fitting, the sharp reproof. In the midst of her explorings among questions beyond her understanding, the Church pulled her up short.

For Liszt the only ritual was the ritual of Bayreuth—secondary to that of the Church—and to that he bent the knee without any mental reservation. There could be no stigma in his interest in, and adherence to music which, when all was said, was his true vocation. On the other hand the Princess was matching her brains against the rarest intellects of a Power that brooked no assault upon foundations age-old, and haughty in security. He, for his part, was looking forward towards the apotheosis of his art, when the world would acknowledge the justice of the cause which he had espoused, and, knowing too well the ramshackle scaffoldings of her thoughts, was perturbed that they might come to grief with the faintest breath of ridicule. Fantastic and eccentric she might be : in her writings, however, he wished to protect her from herself, from folly that heightened her grotesqueness. It is clear that it was her polemics, her disputations, that led eventually to discordance, far more than Liszt's allegiance to the Bayreuth idea. Wagner's invitation had broken silence.

It is noteworthy that from that event, and the years 1872 and 1873, friction and irritability became more marked in Liszt's correspondence with the Princess. In March, 1873, he declared that on two points he differed from her, seriously for him, namely, Weimar and Bayreuth, but on April 11, he added a third point, Rome, with the comment, " Unfortunately I can't write more to you without thinking things out." Can it be believed that in his close intimacy with Hohenlohe, his only friend, the Princess's writings and opinions were never discussed ? The Cardinal's touch seems to peep through the lines of the next letter, five weeks later (May 17).

" Let's talk of the title of your last work. I confess it strikes me as almost rash, but as I am not a competent judge in such matters, I have confidence in your wisdom, which will not have failed to be enlightened by sound advice. It would appear that the researches into the *Causes intérieures de la Faiblesse extérieure de l'Église* do not seem opportune to-day in the eyes of personages who stand high in the confidence of the Holy Father. They are right in thinking that the ordering and decision in Church matters belong exclusively to them. Since you have the additional misfortune of being a woman, you must in this instance resign yourself to the rôle of silence which St. Paul imposed upon your sex. Notwithstanding social courtesies and charming conversation, the ecclesiastical authorities adhere to the same maxim. Learned and saintly women before and after Saint Catherine of Sienna have spoken. Follow their example with admirable ardour and devotion. These, I hope, will be duly recognized when the dark clouds about the Vatican shall have disappeared. But if unfortunately things turn out differently, you have only to submit and humbly obey, for that is the first duty of catholics, beyond all hesitation and discussion."

The advice came too late, for by that time her books were in the printer's hands, so we have Liszt writing on July 18, 1873, " En attendant, Éljen, Hoch et Vivat à vos volumes de près de 1,000 pages chacun ! "

Towards the end of the month he was at Bayreuth, but he returned to the *Causes* on the 7th of August.

" Last evening I read the first fifty pages of your

Causes intérieures which the Cardinal has highly praised. With my admiration is mixed a little stupefaction and even—dare I say it?—fear. The striking and for the most part well-chosen title, however, is giving me some anxiety. . . . I will read line by line the 1,277 pages of your two volumes, and then will talk to you very humbly and at length. I take it that Hohenlohe has already told you of his feelings of approval in a general sense. May I say that I feel the making public of your book should be done with extreme caution on your part? Consequently you should limit yourself to sending out a small number of copies, and with covering letters. Although the title-page hasn't your name, it is known that the work is by you. M. de Werthern, the Prussian Minister at Munich, said so to Hohenlohe without beating about the bush."

Evidently Liszt was giving serious attention to this "stupendo libro," as he called it, but the Cardinal, in spite of his guarded approval, was not by any means favourable to its being circulated openly. By the end of August Liszt had discovered that the first two volumes lent themselves to reflection, and above all provoked controversy.

It is difficult to grasp the whole content and texture of these letters to the Princess, for they are only the fringe of a large subject. There are references to her correspondence with other people the clues to which are obscure. The reconstruction, therefore, of a situation or an episode depends largely upon the directness of Liszt's expressions and his categorical statements in reply to what evidently was the Princess's catechism or her fault-finding.

In this letter of August 31, from Weimar, it would appear that after a superficial glance at the *Causes* Hohenlohe may have praised the work, but on reflection may have been more politic in his criticism of some passages. As a prelate he may have felt it at variance with his office to discuss a question of authority with a lay person and especially with a woman. The Princess may have taken umbrage at something he had written and sent him a tactless and possibly an offensive reply. This may account for Liszt's advising the Princess to give the Monsignore time to recover from his indignation and resentment. His words were, "Je pense que Hohenlohe ne se plaindra pas d'attendre un peu que vous répariez son dommage."

Liszt could not refrain from bringing up the subject of the *Causes*, for again, in September, he said, "you have accurately guessed the 'cause intérieure' of my insisting on keeping the two volumes in question, and I am glad that this discord has been happily resolved, thanks to your forecast. . . . Most explanations only lead to misunderstandings, or to compromise—always necessary in business and politics, but saddening in the inner life of the heart."

Causes Intérieures—Bondage

Writing at Christmas, 1873, he asks for news of the third volume of the *Causes*, but he adds, "You don't think me worthy of it." However it arrives, 1,149 pages of it, and in January, 1874, he speaks with admiration of her great militant mind which he is following timidly and not without some fear. But nine days later (January 31), he receives a shock, and writes, "Since you command me, I'll say nothing more about the *Causes intérieures*, the third volume of which would be better if it were in two. You are unjust in thinking that your ideas and their prodigious development are unpleasing to me and are drawing us apart. Intellectually I am always near you."

So the subject had to be dropped till June, when he took up his abode at the Villa d'Este, and remained there for the most part till February, 1875.

As we are supplied with only twenty-one letters in these eight months, Liszt must have been frequently in Rome. He must have deplored finding her housed as already described, wondering what there was in this creature, as untidy and slipshod in her way of living as in her books, to have so firm a hold over him. Barely settled in the Villa d'Este, he had to weather the storm of her reproaches. Probably he left her without a word, for it was only on the rarest occasions and under the deepest provocation, that he allowed himself an angry retort. It must have been after some "scene" that he wrote to her on June 14, 1874, from the Villa d'Este. From his letter can be gathered the nature of the attack.

He said that he had never expected or wished for any position or promotion in Rome. (In an earlier letter, February, 1874, he had declared that he did not go hunting after ribbons, performances of his works, praise, distinctions, and articles in newspapers.) He then continued to assert that if he had been appointed to the Sixtine Chapel he would have accepted the post in order to render some service to religious art, an erroneous idea perhaps, but without any illusions about the difficulty and worries of such a task. The absence of these things laid no burden upon him : on the contrary it alleviated what he had to bear. Consequently he was making no sacrifice in the matter, and as his inward liberty had for long been assured, he was not under the necessity of seeking what he already possessed. It was absolutely contrary to his nature to indulge in recriminations and to wallow in barren regrets. He knew of them only by hearsay, and no one in the world could reasonably accuse him of them or find any evidence of them in his words, deeds or gestures. Once again, he repeated, he was only too grateful for the courtesy and kindness which many had shown him and were still showing him. In any case he didn't forget the sound maxim : 'To pity one's self is absurd : to be pitied is humiliating.' Certainly one could deceive one's self as one deceived others, but if that happened to him it would be without his knowledge and against his will. Many people of his acquaintance could bear witness that he was always trying meticulously and sometimes painfully to speak the truth, even to the extent of eliminating the little white lies used in good society. . . . After pointing out that he was not in touch with musical affairs on a large scale, he said, " For my humble part I have mixed myself up in musical matters with the greatest reserve, and only when it seemed to me absolutely necessary. Music cannot be produced without musicians and performances." He then referred to the small number of performances of his works in the past fourteen years and concluded with the words, " I have no ambition to soar like an eagle or a bird of paradise : I keep quiet here on earth and put my trust in the life to come. I must therefore protest humbly and sadly against your misjudgment of me."

This may have satisfied the Princess : we do not know how she greeted Liszt on his next visit to her apartments, at any rate she must have been gratified by Cardinal Hohenlohe's encouraging words, "Depth, Purity, masterly Work," applied to the third volume of the *Causes*. A little later, on Liszt's not hearing from her he asked if she was unwell or if he had committed some fresh misdeed. In one of the last letters from the Villa d'Este at this time he spoke of his pleasure in reading the *Mémoires d'une Idéaliste*, by Malwida von Meysenbug. [See *ante*, p. 127, *n*.]

This strange work, by a lady of advanced views —she was under thirty when it first appeared—is a mixture of idealism, the emancipation of women, and revolution. After the disturbances in Berlin in 1848 and in Dresden in 1849, where Wagner played a supremely ridiculous part,[1] she was expelled from Prussia and for some years lived in England, in London, Richmond and elsewhere, always in association with Russians and people of extreme opinion. She described in detail her emotions on the morning when one of her friends was hung in Newgate for murder.[2] She met Wagner in London while he was conducting the concerts of the Philharmonic Society, in 1855, and though greatly influenced by his prose works, she failed to gain his sympathy. At that time he was himself a refugee, and no doubt had the best of reasons for none too close association with a lady who also had become involved in subversive tactics. When, after some years, she was amnestied, she followed up her *Memoiren einer Idealistin* with *Der Lebensabend einer Idealistin* (first edition, 1898) in which she spoke of her intimacy with the Wagner family, with Liszt, and

[1] See *Richard Wagner as he Lived*, and Chapter VIII.

[2] Liszt in 1874 must have been reading the first volume, published in French at Geneva in 1869. The German original came out in 1877. Both books have appeared in many editions. See the monograph on the authoress by Emil Reicke, Berlin, 1911.

with the Princess Sayn-Wittgenstein. Liszt expressed surprise that she was on friendly terms with Wagner, who had treated her brusquely. "The man," he observed, "who had written *The Ring* and *Parsifal* was exempt from superfluous social observances among acquaintances. Wagner did not comply even with the necessary conventions." He said he yielded to Wagner's superiority, even to his own disadvantage, which he did not admit was actually the case. Malwida's trend of thought may be gathered from Liszt's describing her as the Canoness and Reverend Mother Superior of the Order of Free Thought, and so she lived and died in spite of all the efforts of the Princess to change her views.

To understand the references to the Princess's works it has to be remembered that when she was publishing her *Causes* Rome had not yet settled down to a normal existence. The dogma of the Infallibility of the Pope had been promulgated in 1870, only four years before Liszt took up his residence in the Villa d'Este. The status of the Pope himself was insecure and vast political changes were in the air. The fortifications by the Porta Pia still bore the traces of the bombardment by the Italians in September, 1870, and the breach in the wall through which they entered the City. I myself saw the shell-holes still in the walls. With the division sharply marked between Church and State, caution was all the more imperative in discussing the Church from any but the strictly canonical and orthodox point of view. The title alone of the Princess's prodigious work had more than a tinge of heresy in it, and Liszt was giving her a friendly hint that any " faiblesse " in his Church was unthinkable.

" Your courage and perseverance in your work are truly heroic, as well as the confession of your faith, through all the turmoil of ideas and facts. It is useless to repeat to you that many of your ideas do not strike me as sound, [using the German word *stichhaltig*.] In spite of all my efforts I have failed to see an essentially Christian and specifically Catholic movement in contemporary events."

CHAPTER XVII

CAUSES EXTÉRIEURES—RELEASE

It must have been a relief to Liszt that his official duties in Pest, as President of the National Academy of Music, called him thither. He was in an atmosphere rather different from the deadly septics of many a Roman church, combined with the muddy scepticism of the Princess's unventilated apartments. He was a free citizen of Pest, adored by the nation, and, if he had had a turn for diplomacy, he might have been to Hungary what another great pianist of a later day was to his native Poland.

He was not consistent, however, in saying that none more than he was at one with the blood of Poland, with the Slavonic idea, the Slavonic symbolism, the sentiments and hopes of the Slavonic people. Had he been as sincere in this as he professed to be in other things, he might have changed the face of Europe. As it was, he was attempting to win favour in the eyes of the Princess who had some strain of Poland in her veins. In this respect he was weaker than his brilliant successor who put his country, his nationality, far above personal achievement, and, let us hope, laughed quietly at the lost opportunities and diffidence of him to whom he had looked up as his Master.

But here was Wagner with mind set upon one object, the production of *The Ring* in 1876. Wholeheartedly was Liszt pledged to *his* Cause, the Bayreuth Cause, not quite on the same lines as those of the Princess. Yet, full of it as he was, he had to admit that Wagner failed him. The Wagner concert at Pest to raise funds for the Bayreuth theatre had been a success and the receipts satisfactory, but the man himself was churlish. Banquets in his honour had to be countermanded both at Pest and Vienna. "He refuses absolutely to be bound by any social observances," wrote Liszt on March 11, 1875, and it was left to Cosima to do the honours, to the admiration of her father. A few days later Liszt said he left it to men of letters to explode over the mythology and symbolism of *The Ring* : for his own part he "reverenced profoundly the grandeur and amazing character of this monument whose inspiration and musical form have the most astonishing power and beauty. . . . Hitherto nothing had been written to be compared with it for its sustained sublimity and marvellous richness."

Liszt, well out of reach, had not dropped interest in the *Causes*, for, in the same week, he asked the Princess how the work was progressing, and if she intended to limit it to four volumes. In acknowledging one of her letters in which she had been telling him of her studies, he remarked, " To write a thousand pages on the Episcopacy is a long and serious undertaking ! "

At this time her labours were much in his mind, less out of interest in the subject-matter than of anxiety for her risking censure, if not excommunication. So he was hoping that the " good angels would collaborate with her," inquiring how many thousand pages the *Causes* had run to, and could she finish them by Christmas. A year later, writing from Hanover, and again, after an interval of a week, from the Château de Loo, where he was the guest of the King of the Netherlands, he was invoking the " good angels," no less than three times in a fortnight. The Princess seems to have rejected with some heat Liszt's suggestion of angelic collaboration. She could get on quite well by herself without celestial aid. This, at least, is the conclusion that may be drawn from the Abbé's contrite letter. " It is only with grief that I obey your injunction not to utter another word about the *Causes*. Did I know ever so little about theology and politics I would resist : but my ignorance condemns me to resignation."

This ill-matched pair were oscillating between protests of imperishable love—on Liszt's part, at any rate—and sharp criticism of one another's occupations. Meanwhile we may go back to the year 1875 and leave the bonsangeries.

From the time of his leaving Pest, at the end of March, Liszt's progress had something princely about it, meeting the distinguished men of the day, and entertained as the guest of the King of the Netherlands. He was living in the atmosphere of Courts, and in Weimar in May, in addition to the Grand Duke and Duchess there were the King of Sweden, the Emperor of Russia and Queen Olga of Würtemburg, among whom he took his place through what the King of Sweden called "La Royauté du Génie." He was at his ease, and happily too far away to be cross-examined and catechized, yet he was reminding the Princess of her promise to come to Weimar, but adding that if she had decided not to do so, it would be better not to waste time on empty explanations, but for both to preserve a sad silence.

It was as well that her visit was not paid, for she might have been a kill-joy to Liszt during the performance of *Tristan* in June. All that *Tristan* revealed to him—a work so poignant that he could not conceive what remained for composers of opera to do—would have been shattered by her talk of her "open wound," and for all his staunchness Liszt would have been disheartened.

In freedom from the society of the Princess, in freedom from her conversation which would have been one long litany of grievances against Wagner, Liszt spent a perfect fortnight at Bayreuth in the midst of rehearsals for *The Ring*. He wrote that whatever people might say, Bayreuth was the focus [he used the German *Brennpunkt*] of the art in Germany, a statement which could not have pleased the lady, or his quoting Wagner as saying that the mission of music was to regenerate and revive all the arts of the Nineteenth Century. Surely that was a trespass on her domain.

After Bayreuth and Liszt's resumption of fairly close terms of friendship with Wagner, the Princess feared the wreckage of her schemes. The approaching performance of *The Ring* in August, 1876, might be the climax, she felt, of an estrangement which was germinating beneath the specious surface of compliments and professions of devotion.

Liszt was back in Rome at the Villa d'Este in September, when arguments if not recriminations were resumed. Hence his plea: "Forgive my foolish outbreak last evening. The need to reveal to you the depth of my thought is too vehement to restrain me from offending against good taste. I shall try to correct this, and keep myself in that placid state of mind which is very like blessed indifference" (santa indifferenza). But he was never in the "placid state of mind" for long, for in the same month, in a short note, he was speaking of the sublime grandeur and gentleness of her soul:

that he reverenced her every day, blessed her and loved her in all his strength and weakness.

For all this, the Princess was not above complaining to others, for about this time she wrote to Adelheid von Schorn that Liszt was often dining and supping in the City—too often: that he was not going to Tivoli [the Villa d'Este] that he was playing in charming society and squandering his time. "He hasn't lost his creative powers, but his desire to work; and that is the sad result of these five last sad years." She was remonstrating with him as well, as may be gathered from his letter of January 1, 1876, written from the Villa. "Madame Minghetti is a thousand times right in finding that I waste my time in drawing-rooms. I will give up this shameful habit." He had been overdoing the non-clerical part of his status as Abbé.

Sudden changes from exasperation to humility appear in this correspondence. After the first performances of *The Ring*, the Princess must have assailed him for his enthusiasm about the work, about Wagner and about Cosima, for he replied from Weimar on September 6, "in all humbleness I cannot believe that I deserve the letter which I received from you to-day. In the greatest grief and sincerity I hold to what I told you in Rome—that you deceive yourself gravely about your daughter, my daughter and myself. God knows that for many a year my only task was to alleviate your sufferings.

It would appear that I have succeeded badly. For my own part I wish to remember only the hours in which we have wept and prayed together, two hearts in one. After your letter of to-day I give up the idea of returning to Rome."

This must have given the lady pause. She was in a more conciliatory mood for Liszt to have written, ten days later, " Your last letter is full of kindness and indulgence. I thank you with all my heart which still bleeds from recent injuries. Leave me to recover alone, without further discussion of my faults and unreasonableness."

To this we have the dates, the 18th to the 21st of September, but not her letter. On the 26th, Liszt put his position plainly. " My reply would be quite simple if I could make up my mind to return to Rome in October. Don't insist upon it. Besides, I need some months for my complete recovery : and in the first instance I have not the courage to see you. . . . I shall do my best in Hungary not to try my real friends too much and to behave so as to win their approval. Do not judge me too harshly but grant me some charitable indulgence." She must have been overwhelming him with complaints and strictures.

Estimated alone by his self-expression in his letters to the Princess, Liszt's portrait of himself is by no means flattering : at times it is pitiable.

On March 14, 1876, he read in the newspapers

of the death of Countess d'Agoult. This is how he allowed himself to write of her. "Short of hypocrisy, I wouldn't weep more over her death than over her life. Larochefoucauld has truly said that hypocrisy is homage paid to virtue: but it is permissible to prefer true homage to false. Now Madame d'Agoult had pre-eminently the taste and even the passion for the false, except in certain moments of exaltation of which later she could not bear to be reminded."

Yet this side of his nature was so impervious to magnanimity that he could say this to the Princess, the successor of Countess d'Agoult, and be so self-absorbed only a week later as to send to the Princess this unctuous note: ". . . The end of the Pater [Noster] is almost enough for me, ' Forgive us our trespasses as we forgive those that trespass against us.' I will add from my heart the beautiful exclamation of Saint Theresa, ' O God! Pity those who have themselves no pity!' laying my trust simply in the God of pity and mercy."

In Liszt's character there was what might be called " religious snobbery " in strange contrast with the asperity which he displayed in his references to the Countess d'Agoult. May there not be applied to him the very words which he applied to her, " poses et mensonges " ?

Although he was rarely at a loss for some devotional expression when writing to the Princess, it is clear that the last ten years of their lives were clouded by misunderstandings and acrimonious discussions. She might prohibit him from reading her books, but she could not prevent him from hearing them criticized. As he was in close touch with the clerical party he must have had many a hint to bridle his controversial friend. He foresaw catastrophe and was attempting to convince her of her danger before it was too late.

In January, 1877, he began a letter with " Don't let us discuss devotional practices," and then he is more outspoken. " The melancholy burden of my old age is to find our opinions contradictory. That was not so from 1847 to 1862. Except some differences about literary points and my follies, we were wholly in agreement on all essential questions. Rome and your transcendental mind have changed all that. All the same I admit only differences of opinion, but I will never subscribe to differences of sentiment, no matter how flatly I may have to contradict you. To chatter any more about our differences in Rome seems to me superfluous and worrying. Since the *Syllabus*, to which I adhere and submit according to the duty of catholics, we have been in constant controversy over the affairs of Rome, Pest and Weimar." He concludes : " The truth is, and most grievously for me, that four salient reasons keep me away from Rome. Shall I mention them? Yes— they are yourself and myself, your daughter and mine."

We have seen why she took umbrage when Liszt resumed his relations with Wagner and Cosima. Although he refers to the Princess's daughter, neither he nor Adelheid von Schorn throws any light upon their differences. It is not unreasonable to conclude that her daughter, married happily to a young officer holding an important post at the Austrian Court, did not see eye to eye with the Princess, living, as we have seen, in an atmosphere—in two, in fact—that must have been revolting.

After repelling a charge of ingratitude, Liszt returns again to the great work. "What would interest me most of all would be to read the five complete *feuilles* [? sections or pages of a review] on the *Causes*. You are wrong to keep them from me. If my ignorance warrants your isolating me from your literary and philosophic works, I submit to this humiliation only with the deepest sorrow. Formerly in better times, in Weimar and in Rome even, you were more generous to me." Three months later he repeated his complaint that for a dozen years she had not allowed him to share her almost superhuman works.

Then the blow fell. On July 17, 1877, the Sacred Congregation of the Index Expurgatorius issued its decree prohibiting the circulation of the *Causes* among the clergy. It had been published privately and anonymously, but the Cardinals and Bishops did not surrender their copies. It was the fifth volume which incurred the displeasure of the censor, but the Princess went on with the other nineteen, completing the twenty-four within a few days of her death, in 1887.

Liszt naturally was full of sympathy, but after having been kept in the dark for so many years as to the substance and trend of the *Causes*, was helpless in giving advice. She, on her part, was incapable of keeping off contentious subjects. "Some conversations," he wrote at the end of 1878, "step upon pin-points, sometimes on hot coals," and on December 23 he wrote less metaphorically. "Your Roman ways have led you into the bad habit of absolutism, which vetos all discussion. The most discreet and respectful remarks seem to you to be lacking in deference, to be outrageous. . . . It isn't society that causes the divergence of our points of view but your own daughter and also slightly mine. When I am dead you will realize that my soul was and remains ever profoundly attached to yours."

By March, 1882, she had completed twenty-two volumes of the *Causes*. "What knowledge, inspiration, an ardent zeal for the House of the Lord they contain," he exclaimed. "With what dexterity you expose and develop with a masterly hand the themes and hypotheses of politics, administration, organization, hierarchy, discipline and reform of the Church."

But although he compared her with a string of

saints, and called her a prophet foretelling the great future of the Church she must have replied with a bad grace, for he wrote on October 29, 1882, "I hope you deceive yourself in imagining that I am opposed to what you are doing, or that I am out of sympathy with your writings, whatever they may be. In truth I understand nothing of politics or theology: consequently three-fourths of your work is quite beyond me. As for aesthetics, I confess that up till now I have not found the thread of Ariadne which will rescue me from the labyrinth of the numerous systems of philosophers, ancient and modern. Let us hope that at last I shall grasp the true thread in your theory expounded in your *Emotions and Sensations*. Till then I see myself condemned to sorrowful scepticism."

His final reference to the *Causes* is in a letter of February, 1885, in which he tells the Princess of Cardinal Haynald's opinion—that no writer, whether ecclesiastical or lay, equals her amazing expert knowledge. If this were so, why, then, the Index? we may ask.

CHAPTER XVIII

SECRET SERVICE

Of all the Princess's friends in Weimar, the most steadfast was Henriette von Schorn, née Stein, a former lady-in-waiting to the Grand Duchess of Meiningen. She it was who alone stood by the Princess at the Goethe-Schiller ceremony mentioned on p. 61. She refused to follow the example of the other Weimar ladies, and bravely challenged public opinion by keeping on terms of intimacy with the Princess and her daughter, and with Liszt. From the time when the Princess left Weimar for Rome, in 1860, Madame von Schorn corresponded with her till her death in 1869, when her daughter, Adelheid took up the faithful pen.

While the Princess was in Weimar, she had exercised control over Liszt so completely that she had sterilized all initiative on his part except in musical affairs. Left to himself he would have drifted into untidy ways, or would have welcomed the first woman who slipped into his life to see to his comfort and well-being. It was prudent, therefore, that the Princess should be assured that some one whom she knew and trusted was at hand in the rôle of guardian angel, one of that angelic host that tended Liszt in his spiritual home. Those of his earthly home, for all their flights, had no wings.

If Adelheid von Schorn was at first Liszt's " Providence," according to her pet-name, arranging his rooms in the Hofgärtnerei in Weimar—the Altenburg being in other hands and its furniture and contents stored in a by-street—looking after his servants, his meals, keeping him company when he desired it, taking with an ill grace a hand at whist—for Liszt was an inveterate card-player, but rarely for stakes except when they were very low—if, indeed, she discharged her responsibilities in this personal fashion, she was to become, in another fashion Evidence rather than Providence.

At first no doubt she was guarded in her letters to the Princess, but Carolyne knew her Liszt well enough to be certain that he could not remain " unattached " for long, Abbé or no Abbé. Just about the time when Adelheid's mother died there appeared two women who were to give the Princess some concern.

One was an old pupil, Countess Janina. Because of her beautiful handwriting Liszt had entrusted some of his manuscripts to her to be copied—manuscripts which finally she burnt out of revenge. But this was merely a side-issue. Like many another of her sex she had marked down Liszt for her prey, and until she went to America three years after playing one of Liszt's Concertos at a concert in Pest, she gave him no peace. In Pest, in Rome, in Weimar there were incredible scenes in which poison and pistols appeared side by side with threats of suicide and assassination. To make things as bad as they could possibly be, she published (under the appropriated name of Robert Franz, that mildest of composers) two pamphlets, *Souvenirs d'une Cosaque*, and *Mémoires d'une Pianiste*, in which Liszt was depicted with the scantiest disguise. Malicious enough they were, but she was determined to stab Liszt to the heart, so she sent copies to all his friends, including the Pope himself. The gravity of the scandal was increased by Liszt's being within the pale, and it was only through his well-known association with the priesthood and with his friend, Monsignore Hohenlohe, that serious consequences did not result.

Liszt summed her up in his letter to the Princess of May 10, 1871, from Weimar. " For years she has fed her mind exclusively on the most perverse theories and sophistries. Blasphemy, imprecations, extravagances of Proudhon and the new atheistic school, agamist and anarchist, are her familiar litanies."

It is not on record how he got rid of her—probably not by the device mentioned on page 42, in connection with a less reputable but equally violent lady.

The other person whom the Princess had in mind was Baroness Olga Meyendorff, now a widow, whom he had met in Rome some years before as the wife of a Russian diplomat. She was eventually to be to Liszt in Weimar as the Princess was to him in Rome—as the Janina had tried to be in Pest. Very clearly she suggested that Liszt should become the guardian of her orphan sons, and as their education was essential, surely no better school than the Weimar Gymnasium could be found. So all proceeded according to her plan. Amy Fay, in her well-known book, described her as tall and thin, extremely distinguished and graceful. Her dressing always in black won for her the name of the Black Cat—as cold as the Arctic or as burning as the Equator. Less seems to be known of her relations with Liszt than of his with his other friends. The secret has been well-kept. Their correspondence has not been made public.

Liszt's cloth was not the whole armour: it was not thick enough to turn aside the arrows shot at his heart by slender fingers, but in this instance the fingers had claws. So the Baroness Olga was his faithful companion on many a concert-expedition during the rest of his life.

That may not have mattered to the Princess so much as the rumours of Wagner in Bayreuth, and her anxiety that this much talked-of theatre of his might eclipse the opera-house at Weimar. As the day of the laying of the foundation-stone at Bayreuth drew near, she had fears lest the ceremony might prove the occasion for a reconciliation between Liszt and Wagner, and she would not have been herself had she not extracted a promise from Liszt not to be present. He yielded: it was his last sacrifice to her delusions.

That she could not leave the matter alone is shown by Liszt's letter to her after the event. "Your appreciation of Bayreuth is mixed up with some errors of fact. For instance, that Wagner did not invite me. The truth is that he did so in an elegant letter."

Her reply is not given, but its contents may be gathered from Liszt's. "My old bruises (meurtrissures) have hindered me from talking to you about the Bayreuth question. Here is the copy of Wagner's letter and my answer.... For several months I have not written to Cosima at all. Her letters which von Bülow and Madame Moukhanoff have communicated to me, persuade me that it is better that I should not efface myself from her life." The Princess may have felt that on this, as on other occasions, she had blundered, for Liszt speaks of her "grande lettre sur Bayreuth," and proceeds, "It is truly great in the sentiments which inspire it, which I share to a certain extent, not contrary to justice, for justice holds the scales and has to weigh " [impartially].

But that there had been a serious misunderstanding, if not the peril of a rupture, is shown by Liszt's last words in this letter. " On my knees I implore you to believe firmly that all serious disagreement between us is impossible, and that I shall try with all my strength to become entirely of your heart."

At this time it is significant that the Princess was writing to Adelheid that Bayreuth was to her " une plaie vive," remarking that her lively descriptions made up for what Liszt no longer was writing or talking about. . . . " And so you're going to Bayreuth ! Of course you won't talk about me there : that goes without saying. And of Liszt as little as possible." Later on Adelheid was instructed to resort to duplicity. " Prenez donc peu à peu possession de son intérieur."

She was in the position of intermediary when intercourse between Weimar and Bayreuth was established, and as Liszt's emissary was present at the laying of the foundation-stone of the theatre in May, 1872. She was flattered by this confidence which brought her in contact with distinguished people. By humouring her the Princess was acting up to the title of one of her books, " Simplicité des colombes, prudence des serpents." At first Adelheid seemed unconscious of the part she was playing, and innocently was writing to Carolyne in the belief that Liszt and she were always on the best of terms, though she could not shut her eyes to his weaknesses. At the same time, she was witness of the renewed friendliness between him and Wagner, in ignorance that Bayreuth was abhorrent to the Princess and Wagner the blackest of bêtes noires.

At all events Liszt had the courage to discuss the forbidden topic, but the Princess's " old sore " broke out again with the first performance of *The Ring*, about to take place in 1876, and the newspaper accounts of the revolution in stage-craft that the new Bayreuth theatre was to bring about. Adelheid evidently was not able at all times to satisfy the Princess, for she herself made this comment: " Although I have given the Princess plentiful details about the Bayreuth festivities, she has not found them sufficient or to her mind. In conversation it was often difficult to see eye to eye with her : it will be clear that in writing it was still more difficult."

The Princess was in dread lest the breach between Liszt and Wagner should be healed. She was on the alert for any sign that might be interpreted as disloyalty on the part of Liszt towards her, and she was resolved that neither Weimar nor Rome should surrender to Bayreuth. Hence she was emboldened to write to Adelheid as follows, from Rome on August 4, 1876. Her words have truly a Russian flavour.

" . . . You guess what I am still expecting of

you? My letter will reach you a little after you have left Bayreuth. Before the end of August tell me everything that you have seen and heard there. Especially tell me what the newspapers don't report. Unfortunately, dear child [Adelheid was then 37!] as far as correspondence is concerned you are indeed the daughter of a lady-in-waiting. It is evident that you have been brought up in the atmosphere of Courts! You understand me? I wish only to mean by that, that you confine your letters to ordinary things for anybody to read. That is quite frank, and I would not tempt you away from so excellent a habit. All the same a slight exception can be made for an old friend. For a long time I have been accustomed always to return [to their writers] letters containing anything special. In Russia that is the custom. It is an understood thing. In this way both [correspondents] are satisfied: one knows what he needs to know: the other is certain not to have any trouble. There—I have said it. Do as you please: everything of yours is dear to me—your words or your silence."

In plain language the Princess was suggesting that Adelheid should act as her spy, released from any scruples of loyalty towards Liszt, in order to report everything, whether to his credit or his detriment. This letter, in fact, explains the " Prenez donc peu à peu possession de son intérieur." " Gradually worm your way into his confidence, dear Adelheid!"

we can imagine the Princess saying. Though it was thirty years since she had turned her back on Russia, she had not forgotten the methods of the Ochrana or the agent provocateur.

How far this deliberate system of espionage was carried is not clear. Adelheid was in a strategic position, living opposite the Hofgärtnerei, a house furnished by the Grand Duke and Duchess " d'un luxe Wagnérien," an expression which shows that Wagner's tastes had become proverbial. Everybody and everything that went in and out of Liszt's house could be seen by her. At first and for some years she must have been of great use to him while he was in Weimar, acting as his secretary, arranging dates and engagements, writing his letters and interviewing visitors. Frequently he relied upon her to give the Princess full accounts of the musical events in which he took part or was interested, contenting himself with writing short notes to her. There is nothing in his correspondence to show that he suspected Adelheid of breaches of faith, but by his use of the word " Aufsichtsbehörde " he showed himself aware that he was under supervision, and that there was little that he could do or say, that there were few people that he could meet, that there was nothing in the course of his daily life that did not form a report to the Princess. So he dismissed the " Board of Control," and broke off all relations with Adelheid von Schorn.

The most that he allowed himself to write to the Princess (from Weimar, July, 1885) was that he had to cast Adelheid adrift—" laisser vaguer et voguer à son gré "—while recognizing her excellent qualities and not failing in sincere affection for her.

CHAPTER XIX

THE SHRINE

If Liszt was able from time to time to take refuge in Weimar and Pest from the fanaticism of Rome, he was ultimately to find himself surrendering to the fanaticism of Bayreuth of which to a large extent he had been the begetter. The Princess herself remarked that people there lived in such a fanatical world that they would never understand her. We have seen how she intervened to prevent Liszt's being present at the laying of the foundation-stone of the theatre, and how she humbled him by insisting on seeing Wagner's letter of invitation and Liszt's reply. Since 1867, when Liszt went to Triebschen to remonstrate with his "terrible daughter" for having left her husband, von Bülow, till Wagner's invitation—in these five years there was silence between the two men.

There followed the visit to Weimar of Wagner and Cosima in 1872, after the laying of the foundation-stone. In 1875, Liszt was in Bayreuth for the first rehearsals of *The Ring*, and again in 1876 for the first performance of the complete work.

These steps thwarted all the Princess's hopes. Although Liszt persisted in his outpourings of affection the breach was inevitable, and from the quotations given in Chapter XVI it is evident that there was irritation on both sides. Wagner had become an obsession to her in spite of the twenty years since they had last met. Unforgiving and unforgetting, she could never bring herself to see that morally she had been not a whit better than Cosima, and that Liszt to her own husband had been exactly as Wagner had been to von Bülow. Nothing on earth, including the Vatican, could alter that fact. Besides, in the relationship of Cosima to Wagner there was a further parallel in her relationship to Liszt. Both women were masterful—with a difference.

The Princess played upon Liszt's weakness, his desire for peace, his shirking controversy in all things outside music, his religiosity which, she convinced him—and herself—made for righteousness. It was this gentleness in his nature, which might have been mistaken for an attitude of mind too indolent to exert itself, that gave the Princess authority over him.

Cosima, too, was masterful, but it cannot be denied that when she took the definite step of associating herself with Wagner, she made another man of him. It is true that it was not through her that *Tristan* or *Die Meistersinger* saw the light, or indeed

LISZT IN 1886

Photograph by Nadar, Paris

The Shrine

the greater conception to *The Ring*, which had been in his mind when she was a little girl of eleven, but she retrieved him from disorder and arrived on the scene when the drama was sadly in want of a dénouement.

Both women had a streak of vindictiveness in their characters. We can believe that it was some unbridled impertinence on Wagner's part that led the aristocrat, " the slightly vulgar aristocrat," brought up in the Russian Court, to cherish a resentment which with the years attained the stature of hatred. In his commerce with the world, men of his own standing must many a time have had the soft answer trippingly on the tongue, when they discovered how to deal with that ill-conditioned bundle of self, and, for all his failings, his moral and financial unscrupulousness, there must have been something in his fibre to attract and hold men so varying in mental calibre as Richter, placid in his rotundity, Levi, a tangle of nerves, Humperdinck, with nothing of the fairy about him, and the serene Mottl. With Bülow it was different.

In Cosima the vindictiveness took a strange twist. She does not seem to have been endowed with the filial instinct. In the early years of her life her father was no more to her than a name in the newspapers: her mother a cipher. She was too young to be clear in her mind as to her position in regard to her parents. Yes, no doubt, they *were* her parents, and the cautious Anna, Liszt's mother, must have been hard put to it many a time to veil the delinquencies of her son from his sharp-witted daughter. The truth is that Liszt did not possess the rarest gift of all, the gift of fatherhood. It was all very well to be the legal parent—the physiological parent, if you will—but Cosima had conceived her own idea of her father, and it was not altogether in his favour. All this Abbé business, this trying on of soutane, the purple splash of canonry for the photographer, the tailoring of the habit of the Third Order of St. Francis—these were recorded in her brain, not to be forgotten. Prejudiced, narrow in her strong-mindedness as she has been represented, she held the key, and the key was Richard Wagner. She had scorned her father's advice: she had made the sacrifice which was to wound two of Wagner's best friends. She never thought of them, but went her way, emboldened by the assurance that time would justify if not sanctify her step. The success of Bayreuth was to her everything: Liszt was a guest, a stranger, a forestiere, a ξένος.

With von Bülow things had changed, and this was a blow. Whether he felt that Liszt had not taken the active part that he should have done in the Cosima-Wagner affair, or that his artistic views had undergone a drastic revision is not known. The personal element probably was as strong as the musical. Whatever the reason, he was now found in the camp of those who opposed Liszt, supporting with all his influence Brahms and Joachim, and to a less extent Wagner himself. Let this be laid to his credit for magnanimity.

Joachim had seceded some years before, to be reconciled in 1880 with a whisper that he had been in the wrong all the time. Schumann and Mendelssohn were dead: the " glorious and embittered " Berlioz, in spite of his name, Hector, had gone down before Wagner, the Achilles. They, and many another, had emptied Liszt's heart, and Wagner alone was left to fill the dreary vacuum. In Bayreuth Liszt was trying to recreate some of the enthusiasm that had brought about the frail and uncertain alliance with Wagner, and seeking to recover some part of himself that he had cast abroad so prodigally. There may have been a little gratification when Wagner pointed to him in his speeches as the great inspirer, the devoted pioneer, the bearer of the banner with the strange device.[1] Words, merely, or an abiding testimony. Wagner had achieved the end for which he had toiled, and Liszt, knowing too well the countless hours, the concentration, the infinite patience needed for erecting monuments like *The Ring* and *Parsifal*, was glad in his heart. But there would have been more gladness, gladness more supreme, had he found in Bayreuth a secure anchorage for his last years.

[1] It was Liszt's *Excelsior* that supplied Wagner with the opening bars of *Parsifal*.

Pest had claims, and Hungary never let him forget, nor did he desire to forget, that he was of Hungary. Every year he had to comply with the terms of his appointment as head of the National Academy of Music, to him more of a rest than an irksome task. Weimar, too, rich in memories of past conquests, of gentle courtliness, of one-time perfect understanding with his comrade, the Princess, was crowded with suppliant pupils, till von Bülow at one sweep drove forth from the temple that was the Hofgärtnerei the incompetent and the parasite.

Then there was Rome. It was not to her eternal grandeur that he turned: not to the sign-posts of her immortal story, but to a stuffy apartment under the Pincian Hill in which there squatted, spider-like, his inexorable Fate. As a fly Liszt was a poor specimen of the breed. None more than he had fluttered in entanglements, bruised in escape, with wings scarce healed for the next adventure.

It will ever be a mystery why he, along with Berlioz, the forerunner of the orchestral music of his time, should have been enslaved by a woman who had no music in her soul, but had fettered herself by word and troth to a Church, which, as we have seen, was on the verge of repudiating her. In these days the mephitic mist of the Roman Campagna seemed to be over Liszt, changed by some miracle into the heady odour of incense. From a composer of renown the Princess had converted him into her thurifer. The signs of rift were becoming more and more evident, with impatience and petulance on his part. He wanted music, music that could be talked about, but Rome was barren soil. Above all his mind was in Bayreuth, anxious to be in closer touch with Wagner and the family in Wahnfried. It is not so clear that Wagner, now firmly seated on the throne of his desire, was as ardent as of old.

Some light is thrown on Liszt's attitude towards the advanced orchestration of his day, though there is no indication that he had Wagner in his mind. Referring to his piano sketch of his Symphonic Poem, *Von der Wiege bis zum Grabe* (*From the Cradle to the Grave*), he mentioned that it was not yet scored: he was pleased with the themes which he would probably develop when he came to orchestrate them, "in spite of his increasing antipathy towards obésités polyphones, to which his thinness was ill adapted."

Far more than the *Causes* was *Parsifal* to constitute the line of cleavage between Liszt and Carolyne. Her writings, rightly or wrongly, were felt to be prejudicial to the Church of which Liszt on the surface was an active adherent, and much as it might go against his grain to disapprove of her views and plead for caution, she was there concerned with only one element. With *Parsifal* she was concerned with two: the man Wagner, whom she hated, and *Parsifal* itself, whether written by Wagner or by any other person. That it was Wagner's work was to her a double offence. She detested the man who, in her eyes, was the last person to caricature, as she saw it, the holiest rite of all. Unquestionably justified, she was doubtful of Wagner's sincerity. Had he not once described the ceremony which he had come to stage as " Flitterreligionskomödie " ? Thus, at least, had he written to Mathilde Wesendonck. Yet he applied to Liszt for details about the ceremonial in the Grail scene. He may have argued that his aim was to produce a work of art, not a manifestation of faith, and that he was in exactly the same position as a painter like Velazquez, who could transfer his thoughts from Holy Families to the " Rokeby " Venus, or Rembrandt, whose Danae was hardly a fitting neighbour for a Descent from the Cross.

With the Princess, however, it was the greater sacrilege that Wagner of all people should have conceived such a thing, and she was out-spoken and scandalized when she regarded *Parsifal* as a literal translation of sacred acts, and not as highly symbolical and moving in its presentation. Liszt did not, or would not support her. He was ageing, worried because of the growing dimness of his sight, and ill-disposed to enter yet another field for recriminations. He was tired of dogma according to Carolyne : resentful, as an Abbé, of her intrusion into matters, in which, had he been better read and

The Shrine

informed, he could have guided her. But obsessed by her sophistiquailleries and hair-splittings, and swept by the fringe of the clerical party, she kept on her own highway.

Shortly after his arrival in Pest for his official duties after his visit to Wagner in Venice, he was composing again, which gave him most peace of mind, but "without any illusion as to the poor value of what he was writing."

Three weeks later, February 13th, 1883, Wagner was dead.

How Liszt received the news of Wagner's death has been described by Julius Kapp [*Franz Liszt*, pp. 518-519], and I have given in detail, in *Richard Wagner as he Lived*, an account of Wagner's last days. The attitude of Cosima at this time was incomprehensible. In Venice Liszt had kept much to himself, and possibly it was a relief to him to leave it in January, just a month, as it happened, before Wagner died. It seemed unnatural that Cosima without delay should have demanded of her father the return of all Wagner's letters to him. Still more strange was her aloofness in declining to see him till she visited him in Weimar for the first time three years after Wagner's death. Even when he was in Bayreuth in 1884 for *Parsifal*, he just caught glimpses of her in the semi-darkness of the theatre, smothered (engouffrée) in mourning. He felt deeply the inexplicable estrangement.

As for the Princess, whatever she may have felt or thought when her arch-enemy died, all that we can learn is that she passed indifferently to other subjects when the news arrived. Liszt's references were singularly curt and formal. It was as if he was completely resigned and was beginning to lose interest in human affairs, indeed he went the length of speaking of the will that he had made twenty-two years before. He saw the Princess for the last time at the end of 1885.

In 1886, he made that valiant journey to London for the performance of his *Saint Elizabeth* under [Sir] Alexander Mackenzie at St. James's Hall, and the Crystal Palace; and was received with all the honours, from Queen Victoria downwards. Antwerp, Paris, and Weimar saw him again, and then his last pilgrimage to Bayreuth.

PLATE V

Bühnenfestspi[ele]

100! PARS[IFAL]

Bühnenweihfest[spiel]

Besetzung für Don[nerstag]

Amfortas	Herr Perron.
Titurel	„ Fenten.
Gurnemanz	„ Grengg.
Parsifal	„ Grüning.
Klingsor	„ Plank.
Kundry	Frau Brema.
Erster Gralsritter	Herr Ankenbra[nd]
Zweiter Gralsritter	„ Bucksath.
Erster Knappe	Frln. Mulder.

2 Chöre (So[pran]
Die Brüderschaft der

Ort d[er Handlung]

Auf dem Gebiete und in der Burg der Gralshüter
gothischen Spaniens. — Sodann Klingsor's Zaubersch[loss]
zuge[wendet]

100!

Anf[ang]
Beginn des ers[ten]
„ „ zwe[iten]
„ „ drit[ten]

100. Aufführung!

PLAYBILL OF THE HUNDREDTH

aus Bayreuth.

FAL. 100!

drei Aufzügen.

ag, 19. August 1897.

100. Aufführung!

Zweiter Knappe	Frln. Höfer.
Dritter Knappe	Herr Scheuten.
Vierter Knappe	„ Froneck.
Klingsors Zaubermädchen	Frln. Gleiss.
1 Gruppe.	„ Plaichinger.
	„ Pfaff.
2. Gruppe.	Frln. Pazofsky.
	„ Mulder.
	„ Altona.

t), 24 Damen.
, Jünglinge und Knaben.

diung:
at"; Gegend im Charakter der nördlichen Gebirge des
dabhange derselben Gebirge, dem arabischen Spanien
nehmen.

iten:
es Abends 4 Uhr.
„ 6³⁰ „
„ 8³⁰ „

100!

ANCE AT BAYREUTH OF *PARSIFAL*

[*face p. 178*

CHAPTER XX

THE LAST PILGRIMAGE

On July 21, 1886, Liszt arrived in Bayreuth for the performances of *Parsifal*. He had been there in July, 1884, lodging at 1 Siegfriedstrasse, near Wahnfried. Although he had just accepted the position of President of the Wagner Festival, Cosima did not invite anyone, not even her father, to the Finance Committee meetings.

He arrived ill, coughing perpetually, and went back to his old lodgings. Very tired he lay down, but Siegfried and Eva Wagner took him to Wahnfried for the evening. Every morning Cosima brought him his coffee and then went off to the theatre. On July 23, he was no better, but in the afternoon he went to the first of the *Parsifal* performances. His pupils were arriving, Stavenhagen, Sophie Menter and Siloti among them. He spent Saturday evening, the 24th, at Wahnfried. On Sunday, the 25th, in spite of his feverishness he went to *Tristan*, because he had promised Cosima. He sat at the back of the box in the darkness, doubled up, half asleep, with his handkerchief to his mouth. When the house lit up he came to the front of the box and was greeted with an ovation. It is pleasant to know that the audience remembered him.

The next day, the 26th, the doctor saw him and committed the blunder of prohibiting all alcohol; to which Liszt had been accustomed as a matter of routine.[1]

To make things worse the food was unsuitable and Liszt was left the whole day without a soul near him. Everyone was at the theatre. The only person who seems to have grasped the situation was Lina Schmalhausen, a Weimar pupil, who had acted as secretary and now as nurse.

On the 27th she found him worse: he had not slept all night. Cosima arrived and gave orders that no one was to enter the room. Liszt took to his bed, never to leave it. In the evening there was a big reception at Wahnfried, and nobody gave him a thought. Another doctor arrived on Wednesday, the 28th, diagnosed inflammation of the lungs, and ordered complete rest. This was strictly enforced and Cosima assumed control. Although Lina Schmalhausen and Adelheid von Schorn had often nursed Liszt and understood his constitution, they were abruptly dismissed by Cosima's orders. As she had the theatre on her hands, visits to pay, guests to receive, with receptions every evening, Liszt was left to his gloomy thoughts and feverish dreams.

---

[1] The facts in this Chapter are derived mainly from the circumstantial account in Julius Kapp's *Liszt*, pp. 542 *et seq*.

The Last Pilgrimage 181

On Thursday, the 29th, when everyone was at the theatre, Lina went to Liszt's room to take farewell of her Master. He was delirious most of Friday, the 30th. The doctor came about midnight, followed by Cosima, who only then arrived from the theatre. On Saturday, the 31st, another doctor was called in. Cosima spent the entire day and remained for the night at the bedside.

That night, July 31st, at half-past ten, Liszt was heard to say distinctly, " Tristan," and at quarter-past eleven " his noble heart ceased to beat." Although he was an Abbé, extreme unction was not administered.

On the following day the great banquet was given to those who had taken part in the Festival, and Frau Cosima Wagner was present. During the whole of this Festival not a note of Liszt's music was heard in Bayreuth. No place was there for Liszt in Wagner's sun. In his dying and in his death he was all but forgotten, save by his devoted pupils. How accurate had been his presentiment, " If only I don't get ill here ! " His friends were indignant at the want of respect shown. Bayreuth was decorated and beflagged in honour of the visit of the German Crown Prince, afterwards the Emperor Frederick, but the body of Liszt, huddled into a hastily made coffin, was placed in the hall of Wahnfried, the other lodgers in the house in which he died objecting to the presence of the body.

Liszt was buried on August the third. The parish minister (? Lutheran) pronounced the benediction at Wahnfried, the catholic clergy of Bayreuth joined the procession, the pupils carrying torches. Mottl, Intendant von Löen and Mihalowich were the pall-bearers. There does not appear to have been a Requiem Mass, and in spite of his often expressed wish he was not buried in the habit of the Third Order of St. Francis.

Death was not allowed to interrupt the proceedings of the Festival. It is not known if the Princess was warned of Liszt's serious illness, or if she was in any anxiety about not having heard from him after his last letter to her of the 6th of July. Indifference may have stolen in when she discovered that he had for years been slipping out of her grasp, and defiantly was now in the camp of her life-long enemy. If she had been kept in ignorance until after his death, she might have had a grievance that she had been shorn of the opportunity of having the obsequies attended with Roman pomp and ceremonial with hangings, candles, flowers, Liszt's music and a cohort of Franciscans. She had been cheated of her marriage, that marriage to which Liszt, according to his daughter, had looked forward as to a burial service, and even at the last she had been robbed of what Tennyson, unconscious of the bathos, would have called " a splendid funeral."

Other friends of Liszt seem to have been kept in

The Last Pilgrimage

the dark, for when Baroness Meyendorff arrived at the station with the intention of joining Liszt for the Festival, she was struck by the number of wreaths that had come by train from all parts and learned the news from her cabman. She was present at the burial, with Cosima and Daniela.

What could anyone make of it all? A sick man in his seventy-fifth year going to Bayreuth to see the crowning work for which he had fought for forty years: to see his only surviving daughter: to see his grand-children, all of them his, whether by von Bülow or by Wagner, both sons-in-law: arriving worn out, only to take to his bed with all the town bustling with crowned heads, nobility, nationalities of all kinds—while his daughter was holding court with her receptions, acting the grande dame among the occupants of the Fürstin-loge in the theatre, the self-crowned Queen of Bayreuth. And her father, broken in years, half-blind, torn asunder by an incessant cough, left to himself in a neglected lodging, to reckon up the years and days of his life, and in the end to come to this pass.

Well he knew Bayreuth in festivity. He could count, hour by hour, the cabs on their way to and from the ugly building on the hill: he could hear in his mind the fanfares announcing the beginning of an act: he could imagine the hush as the lights went down and the first chords stole mysteriously from the concealed orchestra. Well he remembered every note of that amazing tissue of sound so that his fevered brain could follow scene after scene, from the Prelude to *Tristan* to the Grail music of *Parsifal*, each well-timed, each climbing up to the great heights, then silence, as Ibsen put it, " Opad, opad, til store Stilhed."

He could remember, only three years before, slipping away from the crowd into the woods to be alone in thought with that more serene nature which brought him into communion with the peace that passeth all understanding, a peace that rarely had been his.

For him no clatter of dishes in a packed and steamy restaurant, with raucous throats shouting down in contradiction the enthusiasm of a neighbour. For him no shibboleths, no phylacteries. As he lay, conscious that his hour was near he cast up, in his moments of wakening, all that he had been to man and to woman. A strange procession must have passed through his mind, linked together waywardly, but still linked, some frail, some solid—Caroline Saint Criq, La Prunarède, Marie D'Agoult, La Dame aux Camellias, Lola Montez, Carolyne Wittgenstein, Olga Meyendorff—who are the others to complete the chain ?—till he was brought up abruptly by a kink, his own daughter Cosima.

In that dreary week of fever and neglect, with all Wahnfried ablaze for receptions, for homage, night after night not far off his window, his own daughter had left him in his loneliness to cough out his very heart, while broken in body and soul he lay hard by, with no one to moisten his dried-up lips. He was the victim of Wagnerian fanaticism.

CHAPTER XXI

FANTASTICS

It is singular that the most discussed composer of his century should have attracted and repelled two individuals as fantastic as himself, and should have developed in one, in Liszt, a kind of fanaticism which a very different fanaticism in the Princess Carolyne Sayn-Wittgenstein could not destroy.

Can it be said that between any two of this amazing trinity the divine gift of friendship could have existed? Between Liszt and Wagner arose the spectre of betrayal: between Liszt and the Princess there were two stumblingblocks, Bayreuth and her meddlings with ecclesiastical affairs: between Wagner and the Princess there was Bayreuth again: there was his acknowledged supremacy in music, and in smaller matters his ill-natured manners and his misjudged dogmatism in concerns about which many a wiser head had kept silence.

Those who have had to study this strange history are wondering that there was no *deus ex machina*, no blunt, down-right intruder, without any notions of art, to burst in upon the trio and give each a

Fantastics 187

slice of his mind. Unfortunately there was none courageous enough to lay Wagner by the heels, to strip Liszt of his soutane, and to drag the Princess into the open air which she abhorred.

Across this stage marched an incongruous procession: royalties and grand dukes, philosophers and pessimists: cardinals and camerlingi, virtuous wives and Aspasias: names remote from music, but who in themselves could have laid the foundations of a history of the period in literature, in thought and in morals.

Amid them, these three beings, in character each the negation of the other, were drawn together by an invisible current to be suddenly interrupted and the circuit left incomplete. To them there seldom seems to have been perfect quietude, each with an angry blot somewhere, each within a hair's-breadth of the goal: one at length to attain it, but only across the wreckage and havoc that he had made.

For none can be claimed serenity. The Princess was killing the soul in Liszt, day by day, inch by inch. Blinded by her specious saving of souls, her mystical exaltations, her morbid introspections, she had not the wit to see that her arid nourishment must surely lead to starvation. Small wonder that he sought the milk of human kindness where it could be found, with the easy tolerance and gait of those well-informed of the ways and fashion of Abbés.

It was all the Commedia del' Arte over again. The

leading lady, the lover, both discomfited by the buffone. Harlequin and Columbine, he in black, she in a flutter of many-coloured ribbons, might trip it fantastically, but the protagonist held the stage.

Yet behind the posturings there was in each a consuming fire to create. For all misunderstandings and asperities, eaves-droppings and censorship, there was a great and abiding loyalty to their aims.

Bigoted and opinionative as the Princess was, and misplaced as her extraordinary efforts might be, she was still steadfast in pursuit of her goal, heedless of advice, intolerant of criticism. No idler was Liszt: witness his vast pianoforte répertoire when he was a mere lad: witness the reams of his compositions, but above all his disinterestedness and championship of all that was highest in his art. Wagner, too, with eyes fixed on the destiny that he knew would be his, was opening up an uncharted realm of music, with aspects and adventures hitherto undreamt.

There was the paradox. There could be no disloyalty to their enterprise. That they kept sacred and remote, far from the commerce of the world.

BIBLIOGRAPHY

Agoult, Marie, Countess d' [Daniel Stern] : *Mes Souvenirs, 1806-1833.* Paris, 1877.

Agoult, Marie, Countess d' [Daniel Stern] : *Nélida.* Brussels, 1846.

Almanach de Gotha, 1855-1865 [Ephemerides].

Auvergne, Edmund B. d' : *Lola Montez.* London, n.d.

Baedeker's Central Italy, 1872-1879.

Bainville, Jacques : *Louis II de Bavière.* Paris, 1900.

Balzac, Honoré de : *Béatrix.* Paris, 1838-1845.

Barthou, Louis : *La Vie amoureuse de Richard Wagner.* Paris, 1925.

Benjamin, René : *La prodigieuse Vie d'Honoré de Balzac.* Paris, [1925].

Bülow, Hans von : Briefe, Leipzig, 1904-1907.

Cabanès, Augustin : *Balzac ignoré.* 2nd ed. Paris, [n.d.]

Combarieu, Jules : *Histoire de la Musique,* Vol. III. Paris 1919.

Du Bled, Victor : *La Société française depuis cent Ans.* Paris, 1st Series, 1923 ; 2nd Series, 1924.

Fay, Amy : *Music-Study in Germany.* London, 1886.

Ferry, Gabriel : *Balzac et ses Amies.* Paris, 1888.

Floyd, Juanita Helm : *Women in the Life of Balzac.* New York, 1921.

Glasenapp, C. F. : *Das Leben Richard Wagners.* 4th ed. Leipzig, 1905.

Göllerich, August: *Franz Liszt.* Berlin, 1908.
Habets, Alfred: *Borodin and Liszt,* transl. by Rosa Newmarch, London, [n.d.].
Hauptmann, Moritz: *The Letters of a Leipzig Cantor,* edited by A. Schöne and F. Hiller. Transl. by A. D. Coleridge, London, 1892.
Huneker, James: *Franz Liszt.* New York, 1911.
Kapp, Julius: *Richard Wagner und Franz Liszt, eine Freundenschaft.* Berlin, 1908.
Kapp, Julius: *Franz Liszt.* Berlin, 1909.
La Mara [Marie Lipsius]: *Liszts Briefe.* Leipzig, 1905.
La Mara: *Letters of Franz Liszt,* transl. by Constance Bache. London, 1894.
Le Breton, André: *Balzac, l'Homme et l'Oeuvre.* Paris, 1905.
Liszt, Franz: ein Gedankenblatt von seiner Tochter. 2nd ed. München, 1911.
Meysenbug, Malwida von: *Memoiren einer Idealistin.* 7th ed. 1903.
Meysenbug, Malwida von: *Der Lebensabend einer Idealistin.* 6th ed. 1905.
Moscheles, Life of, adapted from the original German by A. D. Coleridge. London, 1873.
Newman, Ernest: *Wagner as Man and Artist.* 1st ed. London, 1914.
Pourtalès, Guy de: *La Vie de Franz Liszt.* 2nd ed. Paris, 1925.
Ramann, L.: *Franz Liszt.* Leipzig, 1880.
Schorn, Adelheid von: *Franz Liszt et la Princesse de Sayn-Wittgenstein,* traduit par Mme. L. de Sampigny, Paris, 1905.
Séché, Alphonse and Jules Bertaut: *George Sand.* Paris, [n.d.].

Bibliography

Wagner, Richard : *Briefwechsel zwischen Wagner und Liszt.* Leipzig, 1887. Transl. by F. Hueffer, London, 1888.

Wagner, Richard : *Letters to Wesendonck et Al.* Transl. by W. Ashton Ellis. London, 1899.

Wagner, Richard : *Mein Leben.* English Text. London, 1911.

Wallace, William : *Richard Wagner as he Lived.* London, 1925.

INDEX

Agoult, Charles d', 19, 22, 28
   Liszt "a man of honour," 22, 28, 44
Agoult, Marie d', (Daniel Stern), xiv, 18, 25, 26, 27, 33, 44, 46, 53, 61, 75, 103
   Death, Liszt's comment on her, 154
   Nélida, 44 *et seq.*, 120
   Souvenirs, 22, 119 *n.*
Albert, Prince, 35
Almanach de Gotha, 78, 100
Altenburg, the, 60, 61, 106
Antonelli, Cardinal, 106
Artigaux, Count d', 10
Austria, Empress of, 24, 44

Bach, *B Minor Mass*, 67
Balzac, 20
   His *Béatrix*, 45 *et seq.*, 120
Barberini, Palazzo, 114
Bartin, Abbé, 11
Bayreuth, 122, 133, 135, 137, 138, 148, 151, 163, 164, 165, 169 *et seq.*, 179 *et seq.*
Beethoven, Centenary, 52
   Concerto, 38
   Monument, 4, 28, 31, 32, 42, 48 *et seq.*
   Sonatas, 24
Bellini, 24
Belloni, 40 *n.*, 49 *n.*, 57, 73
Berlin, 38 *et seq.*
Berlioz, xi, 3, 15, 17, 18, 64, 97, 173, 174
   Symphonie Fantastique, 5
Bethmann, Simon Moritz, 19
Blessington, Lady, 35
Boehm, Sculptor, 15
Bonn, 35, 38, 42, 50, 53
Borodin, 125
Brahms, 4, 6, 48 *n.*, 66, 173
Bülow, Hans von, 73, 78, 87, 91, 94, 117 *et seq.*, 122, 123, 171
   His daughters 117, 119

Cancans, philology of, 104 *n.*
Cassel, 37
Cassiat, Countess Valentine, 53
Causes Intérieures, 104, 127, 132 *et seq.*, 143, 145, 147 *et seq.*, 156, 157, 158
Cherubini, 65
Chopin, 15
Cologne Cathedral, 36
Cornelius, Peter, his *Barber of Bagdad*, 4, 65, 79, 104

Delacroix, Eugène, 15
Dingelstedt, 65, 79
Disraeli, his *Lothair*, 120
Dommanget, Dr., 46
Donizetti, 24
Dresden, 41, 42, 63, 69, 78
   Revolution, 70
Dubois, Charles, 41 *n.*

Fay, Amy, 162
Flavigny, Vicomte de, 19
Foyatier, Sculptor, 16

Geneva, 21
George IV, 8
Girardin, Émile de, 20 *and n.*
Goethe, 19, 54
   Monument, 78, 97
Grétry, 65

Hauptman, Moritz,
   His opinion of Bach, 67
     ,,   ,, of Liszt's playing, 64
     ,,   ,, of *Tannhäuser*, 64
     ,,   ,, of Wagner, 64, 84
Haynald, Cardinal, 158
Heine, Heinrich, 4, 15, 40 *n.*, 48, 49 *n.*
Herder, 54

193

Hiller, 53
Hofgärtnerei, the, 160, 167, 174
Hohenlohe, Monsignore, afterwards Cardinal, 113, 130, 136 et seq., 143, 161
Hohenlohe—Schillingsfürst, Prince Konstatin, 57, 100
Hugo, Victor, 15
Huneker, J., 96 n.
Hungary, 24, 29 et seq., 147, 174

Ibsen, 184
Imbert, Hugues, x
Index, the, 104, 156, 158

Janina, Countess, 160 et seq.
Jena, Cathedral, Liszt in, 125
Joachim, 4, 66, 173
Judenthum, das, 98 et seq.

Kapp, Julius, 22 n., 41 n., 48 n., 127 n., 177, 180 n.
Kiev, 54 et seq.

Lamara, 127 n.
Lamartine, 15, 53
La Prunarède, Adèle de, 17, 20, 103
Le Breton, André, criticism of Balzac, 45
Leipzig, 5, 31, 33, 50, 64, 65, 77, 78
Liège, 41 n.
Liszt, Adam, 7, 9
  Anna, 9, 14, 28, 114, 115, 172
  Blandine, 19, 21, 78, 104, 117
  Cosima, birth, 19, 23
    Divorced by v. Bülow, 123
    During Liszt's last illness, 179 et seq.
    Influence over Wagner, 170
    Living with Wagner, 118, 121, 122, 134
    Marriage with v. Bülow, 78, 117
    Marriage with Wagner, 123
    On Wagner's death, 177
    Quoted, 93 n.
    Relations with Liszt, 111, 121, 152, 156, 169, 171, 172, 177
  Daniel, 19, 28

Liszt—continued
  Franz
    Beethoven Monument, 4, 28, 31, 42, 48 et seq.
    Championship of composers, 63, 173
    Correspondence, criticism of, 64, with Princess Wittgenstein, 81 et seq., 95, 103 et seq., 126
    Death, last illness and, 179 et seq.
    Decorations, his, 26, 38, 39, 41, 75, 113
    Freemason, 37
    Friction with Princess Wittgenstein, 111, 135, 137, 140, 141, 142, 146, 149, 151, 152, 153, 155, 157, 163, 164, 170
    Janina, his description of, 161
    Lisztomanie, 30, 37, 39, 40
    Marriage with Princess Wittgenstein discussed, 107, vetoed, 108
    Obituary, his premature, 11
    Police dossier, 25
    Pupils, 21, 174, 179
    Recital, last public, 54
    Religious bent, 7, 9, 11, 58, 89, 102, 103, 154, 170, 174
      Minor orders, 113, 121, 125
      Titular Canon, 136
      Vox Romana, 100, 103
    St. Criq, Caroline, 9, 10, 11
    Separation from Madame d'Agoult, 46
    Sword of honour, 30
    Vagabond indefatigable, 6, 28, 29 et seq., 49
    Wagner, enthusiasm for his music, 74, 105, 112, 145, 152
      Friction with, 79, 97, 122, 169
      Friendship with, 2, 68 et seq., 81 et seq., 88, 90, 134, 151, 156
Wittgenstein, Carolyne Sayn-, See
Wonder-child, 7

Index

Liszt, Franz—*continued*
  Works, references to, Christus, 48 *n*., Dante Symphony, 77, 78, 92, 95, 115; Don Sancho, 8; Excelsior, 173 *n*., Faust Symphony, 77; Festival Cantata, 51; Mass, 77, 93; Mazeppa, 65, 78; St. Elizabeth, 178; Symphonic Poems, 65, 77, 94, 95, 133; Von der Wiege bis zum Grabe, 175; Was ist der Deutschen Vaterland, 38; Zigeuner, die, und ihre Musik in Ungarn, 95

Leipzig, 5, 31, 33, 50, 64, 65, 77, 78
Lohengrin, 4, 73, 74, 79, 94, 132
London, 8, 15, 34, 178
Lothair, 120
Ludwig I, 42
Ludwig II, 42, 43, 75, 83, 85, 112, 117 *et seq*.
Mackenzie, Sir A. C., 178
Meistersinger, Die, 74, 112, 123
Mendelssohn, 4, 32, 33, 39, 48
Metternich, Princess, 48 *n*.
Meyendorff, Baroness Olga, 162, 183
Meyerbeer, 99
Meysenbug, Malwida von, 127 *n*., 144, 145
Milan, 23
Montez, Lola, 42 *et seq*., 44, 51, 103, 119, 121
Moscheles, 52
Munich, 41, 75, 85
Museum, British, 127 *n*.
Musset, A. de, 15

Napoleon III, 53, 75
Nicholson A., flute player, 8
Nietzsche, 97
Nikolaus I, Tsar of Russia, 60
Nonnenwerth, 35, 37

Olliver, Emile, 78, 104, 115
Orsay, Count d', 35
Oven, Charlotte von, 43

Paderewski, 147
Paër, 9
Paganini, 15
Paris, 9, 12, 33, 34, 95, 104, 105
Parsifal, 145, 173, 175 *et seq*., 179 *et seq*.
Patin, Guy, his Maxim, 27
Pest, 135, 147, 174, 177
Pius IX, 104, 110, 113, 130, 145
Pohl, R, 92, 94, 95, 122
Potter, Cipriani, 8
Professorenwirtschaft, 86, 88

Rembrandt, 176
Revolution in Europe, 59
Ricordi, 23
Rienzi, 42
Ring, The, 148, 151, 165, 173
Ritter, Karl, 84
Rohlfs, 127 *n*.
Rome, 26, 35, 100 *et seq*., 137, 145, 174
Römische, Brille, 109
Rossini, 16
Rubini, 49 *n*.
Russia, Liszt sets out for, 40; his caravan, 41, 50; Autocracy, 58, 60, 72

Saint-Criq, Caroline, 9, 20
San Carlo al Corso, 108, 110
Sand, George, 15, 18, 23, 25 *et seq*., 45, 46
Schiller, 54, 78, 97
Schlesinger, 34
Schmalhausen, Lina, 180, 181
Schorn, Adelheid von, 126, 152, 156, 159 *et seq*., 180
Schubert's *Erlking*, 114
Schumann, 4, 5, 32, 33, 48
Secret Service, 159 *et seq*.
Spohr, 37
Strossmayer, Monsignore, 130

Tannhäuser, 63, *et seq*., 69, 75, 104
Thalberg, 23
Tottel's *Paradise*, 128
Triebschen, 83, 119, 122
Tristan, 92, 94, 95, 132, 133, 150, 179, 181

Uhlig, 14

Index

Vatican, the, 60, 108, 138
Velazquez, 176
Venice, 177
Victoria, Queen, 34, 178
Vienna, 24, 30
Villa d'Este, 108, 111, 130, 141, 151, 152
Vox, Romana, 100, 103

Wagner, Minna, 85, 86, 104, 105
Richard,
   Asyl, dismissal from, 79
   Banishment from Bavaria, 83, 119
   Banishment from Saxony, 69, 73
   Bayreuth, 122 (see also)
   Borrowings, musical, 96 *n*., 99, 133
   Bülow, H. von, indebtedness to, 123
   Bülow, H. von, correspondence with, 87, 92, 132
   Cosima Liszt, relations with, see Liszt, Cosima
   Death, 177
   Dresden, appointment in, 69
   Extravagances, 81 *et seq.*, 84, 167
   Grievances against Liszt, 88, 90 *et seq.*
   Hauptmann's criticism, 64, 84
   Jews, hatred of, 82, 98
   Liszt's compositions never performed by, 94, 97, 181
   Liszt, meetings with (Paris), 34, (Dresden) 43, 63, (Weimar) 69 *et seq.*
   Nickname in Munich, 43, 119
   Revolutionary, 69 *et seq.*
   Ritter, allowance from Frau, 84
   Schwärmerei, 68
   Triebschen, 119, 122
   Wittgenstein, attitude towards Princess, 86, (see also)
   Siegfried, 123, 179
Walküre, Die, 86

War, Franco-Prussian, 53, 78
   Seven Weeks', 83
Weimar, 4, 38, 53, 59, 77 *et seq.*, 150
   Dowager Grand Duchess of, 60, 63, 78
   Grand Duke of, 59
Wesendonck, Mathilde, 79, 80, 132, 176
   Otto, 87
Wieck, Clara (Frau Schumann), 32, 33, 38, 66, 67
Wieland, 54
Wittgenstein, Prince Nikolaus Sayn-, married to Carolyne, 56; deserted by Carolyne, 56; obtained divorce from her, 78, 98, 100; re-marriage 101; death, 111
Princess Carolyne Sayn-,
   Clerical party, relations with, 106, 109, 110, 113, 125, 130, 134, 157
   Dévote, 58, 60, 128, 136, 174
   Divorce, 58, 76, 78
   Liszt, meeting, 55 *et seq.*
   Marie, her daughter, 57, 59, 60, 61, 63, 100, 152, 155, 156
   Marriage projected, 102, 104 vetoed, 108, 125
   Personality, her, 62, 102, 125 *et seq.*
   Rome, 102, 126 *et seq.*
   Russian methods, her, 164, 166
   property, her, 57, 61
   Wagner, his bêtises, 74, 76, 79
   hostility towards, 79, 88, 96, 112, 131, 163, 164, 165, 171, 175
   Weimar, living in, 60 *et seq.*, 77 *et seq.*, rebuff in, 61, 77
   Writings, her, 104, 126, 127, 134, 135, 158
   (See also *Causes Intérieures* and Liszt, Franz)
Woronince, 56

Zurich, 81 *et seq.*, 86 *et seq.*

For Product Safety Concerns and Information please contact our EU representative GPSR@taylorandfrancis.com
Taylor & Francis Verlag GmbH, Kaufingerstraße 24, 80331 München, Germany

www.ingramcontent.com/pod-product-compliance
Lightning Source LLC
Chambersburg PA
CBHW062223300426
44115CB00012BA/2191